Word for Windows 6

The Visual Learning Guide

Watch for these forthcoming titles in this series:

Quicken 3 for Windows: The Visual Learning Guide

Available Now!

Windows 3.1: The Visual Learning Guide
Excel 4 for Windows: The Visual Learning Guide
WordPerfect 6 for DOS: The Visual Learning Guide
1-2-3 for Windows: The Visual Learning Guide
WordPerfect 6 for Windows: The Visual Learning Guide

How to Order:

Quantity discounts are available from the publisher, Prima Publishing, P.O. Box 1260BK, Rocklin, CA 95677; FAX (916) 632-4405 . On your letterhead include information concerning the intended use of the books and the number of books you wish to purchase.

Word for Windows 6
The Visual Learning Guide

Grace Joely Beatty, Ph.D.

David C. Gardner, Ph.D.

Prima Publishing
P.O. Box 1260BK
Rocklin, CA 95677

Library of Congress Catalog Card Number: 93-85790
ISBN: 1-55958-395-9

Executive Editor: Roger Stewart
Managing Editor: Neweleen A. Trebnik
Project Manager: Becky Freeman
Production and Layout: Marian Hartsough Associates
Interior Design: Grace Joely Beatty, S. Linda Beatty, David C. Gardner,
    Laurie Stewart, and Kim Bartusch
Technical Editing: Linda Miles
Cover Design: Page Design, inc.
Color Separations: Ocean Quigley
Index: Katherine Stimson

Prima Publishing
Rocklin, CA 95677-1260

94 95 96 RRD 10 9 8 7 6 5 4 3

Printed in the United States of America

CONTENTS

Customize Your Learning

Prima *Visual Learning Guides* are not like any other computer books you have ever seen. They are based on our years in the classroom, our corporate consulting, and our research at Boston University on the best ways to teach technical information to nontechnical learners. Most important, this series is based on the feedback of a panel of reviewers from across the country who range in computer knowledge from "panicked at the thought" to sophisticated.

This is not an everything-you've-ever-wanted-to-know-about-Word for Windows 6 book. It is designed to give you the information you need to perform basic (and some not so basic) functions with confidence and skill. It is a book that our reviewers claim makes it "really easy" for anyone to learn Word for Windows 6 quickly.

Each chapter is illustrated with full-color screens to guide you through every task. The combination of screens, step-by-step instructions, and pointers makes it impossible for you to get lost or confused as you follow along on your own computer. You can either work through from beginning to end or skip around to master the skills you need. If you have a specific goal you want to accomplish now, choose it from the following section.

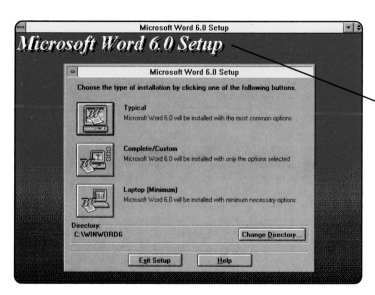

SELECT YOUR GOALS

❖ I would like help installing Word for Windows 6.

Go to the Appendix, "Installing Word for Windows 6."

❖ I'm new to Word 6 and I want to learn how to create and print a letter.

Turn to Part I, "Entering, Editing, and Printing Text," to learn how to set margins, change the font, and enter text. You'll also learn how to save, name, and print a document, and to use the spelling checker, grammar checker, and Thesaurus.

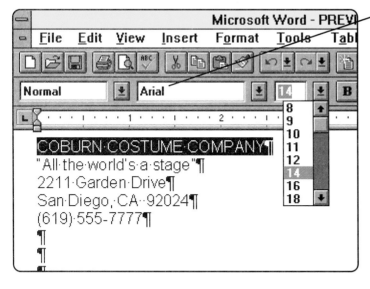

❖ I want to know how to customize a document.

Turn to Part II, "Formatting a Document," to learn how to customize text by changing the type style to bold, italic, and underline. You will add a header and a page number. You will also learn how to center text and create special effects, such as a bulleted list and a shaded border.

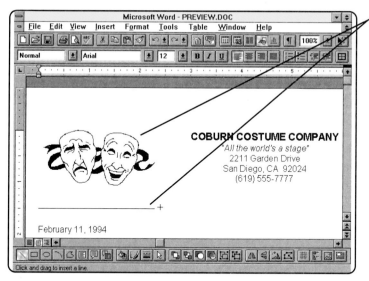

❖ I want to know how to insert pictures into my documents and how to use the draw program.

Chapter 8, "Adding Pictures and Shaded Borders, and Drawing a Line," covers the steps needed to use the library of clip art that comes with Word 6. It also introduces the drawing program by teaching how to draw a line.

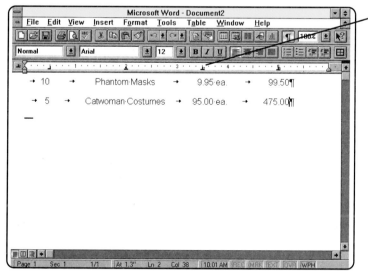

❖ I want to know how to set tabs.

Turn to Chapter 9, "Setting and Applying Tabs."

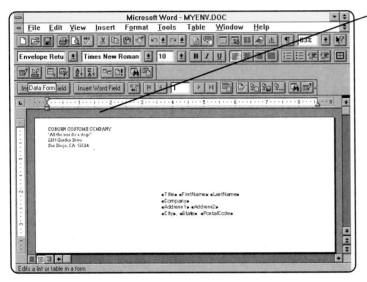

❖ I want to know how to use Word 6's special Envelope features.

Turn to Chapter 12, "Printing Envelopes," to learn how to print a single envelope.

Chapter 15, "Merge Printing Envelopes for a Mailing List," covers how to print merge envelopes.

❖ I want to learn how to create and print a personalized version of a form letter for a list of people.

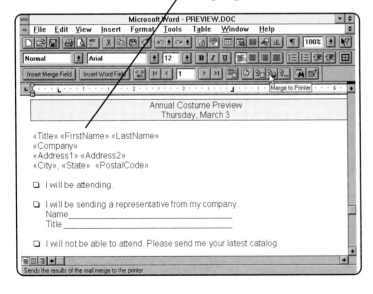

In Chapter 13, you will learn how to create a mailing list. Chapter 14 teaches you how to edit a mailing list and Chapters 15 shows you how to set up and print a personalized version of a form letter.

❖ I want to set up a table.

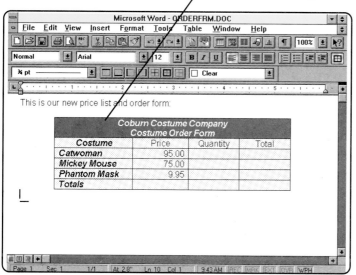

Turn to Part IV, "Introducing Tables," to learn how to create a table, edit a table, and use the AutoFormat to apply specially designed formats.

You will also learn how to open an Excel file in Word.

❖ I want to learn how to use some of the time-saving features of Word 6 that will help improve my productivity.

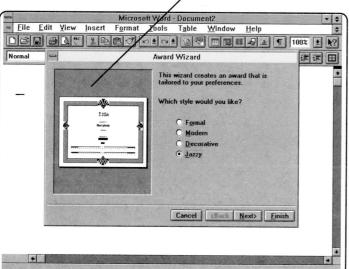

Turn to Part V and learn how to use the Wizard Templates and AutoCorrect. You will even learn how to write your own macro to automate multi-step tasks.

Program Manager

Part I: Entering, Editing, and Printing Text

Changing Margins and Fonts and Entering Text

The philosophy of the *Visual Learning Guide* series is that people learn best by doing. In this chapter you will do the following:

❖ Open a document
❖ Set margins
❖ Change the font and the font size
❖ Enter text
❖ Show paragraph formatting marks
❖ Learn to read the status bar
❖ Use specialized fonts to insert symbols into the text

OPENING WORD FOR THE FIRST TIME

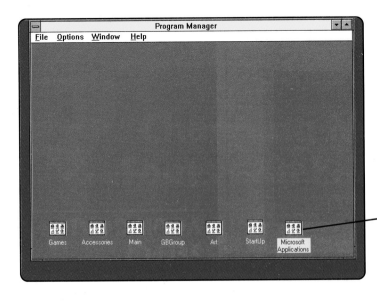

1. **Type win** at the C:\> (C prompt) on your screen to boot up Windows, if it is not already on your screen. Since Windows provides for tremendous customization, you will probably have different group icons at the bottom of your screen than you see in this example.

2. **Click twice** on the **Microsoft Application icon** at the bottom of your screen.

3. **Click twice** on the **Microsoft Word icon**. You will see an hourglass, then the copyright information for Word. Then you will see the opening Word screen with a Tip of the Day on the screen.

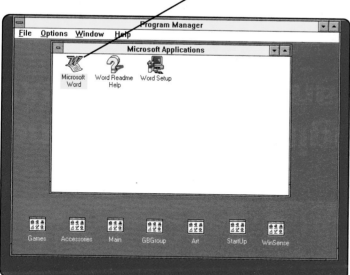

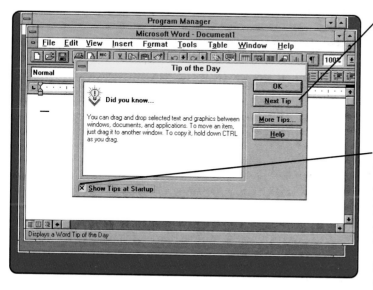

4. **Click** on **Next Tip** to see another tip.

Every time you boot up Word 6, you will see a Tip of the Day

If you do not want to see a Tip of the Day every time you start Word, **click** on **Show Tips at Startup** to remove the X from the box. This will prevent Word from automatically showing tips. If you choose this option, you can still see tips by choosing the Tip of the Day command from the Help menu.

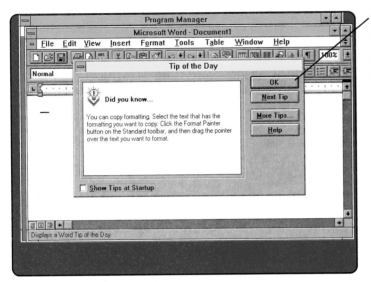

5. **Click** on **OK** to close the dialog box. A blank Word document will appear on your screen.

If your Word document screen does not fill the screen completely, as you see in this example, you can enlarge the screen to give yourself more work room.

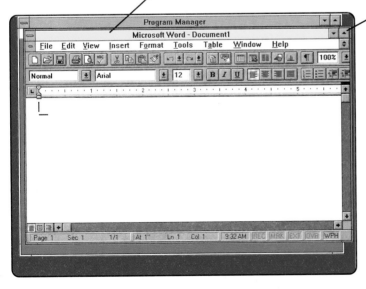

6. **Click** on the **Maximize (▲) button** on the right of the Microsoft Word Document1 title bar. This will maximize Document1 to fill the screen. Your screen will look like the next example.

Notice that the title bar reads Microsoft Word-Document1. This will change when you name the document in Chapter 2, "Naming and Saving a Document."

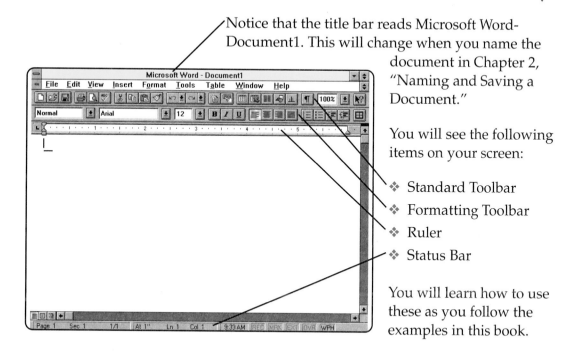

You will see the following items on your screen:

- ❖ Standard Toolbar
- ❖ Formatting Toolbar
- ❖ Ruler
- ❖ Status Bar

You will learn how to use these as you follow the examples in this book.

SETTING MARGINS

The standard (*default*) margins in Word are preset at 1 inch on the top and bottom and 1.25 inches on the left

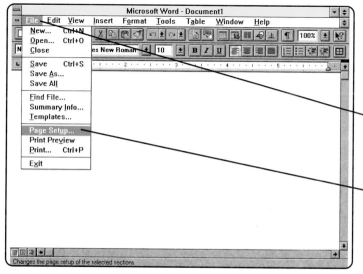

and right. You can change any or all of these. In this example you will change the top, left, and right margins.

1. **Click** on **File** in the menu bar. A pull-down menu will appear.

2. **Click** on **Page Setup**. The Page Setup dialog box will appear.

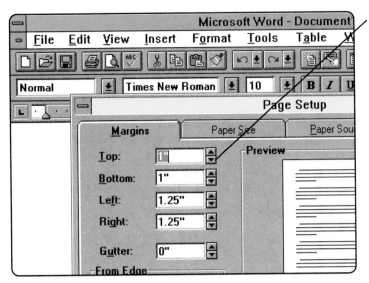

3. **Click twice** on the ▼ next to the Top Margin box. The Top Margin box will change from 1 inch to .8 inches.

4. **Click repeatedly** on the ▼ next to the Left margin until the Left margin is 1 inch instead of 1.25 inches.

5. **Click repeatedly** on the ▼ next to the Right margin until the Right margin is 1 inch instead of 1.25 inches.

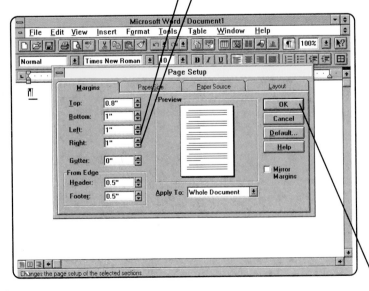

You are making the margins smaller than standard to give yourself extra room to create the letterhead in the example in this chapter. (If you are going to print on stationary that already has a letterhead, the top margin for a short-to medium-length letter should be about 2.5 inches and the side margins should be 1.25 inches.)

6. **Click** on **OK**.

CHANGING THE FONT AND THE FONT SIZE

Word is set to print with the Times New Roman *font*, or type style. In this example you will learn how to change the font.

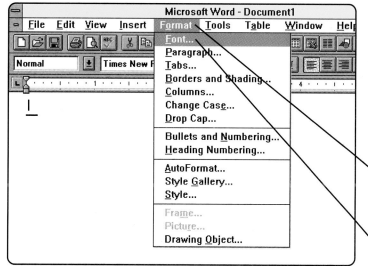

Changing the Current Document Font

1. Click on **Format** in the menu bar. A pull-down menu will appear.

2. Click on **Font**. The Font dialog box will appear.

3. Type the letter **a** to move to the top of the Font list.

4. Click on **Arial** if you would like your letter to look like the sample letter in this chapter. If you prefer to choose another font, your lines may end up differently than you see in the following examples. That's okay. Just be aware that you may see differences.

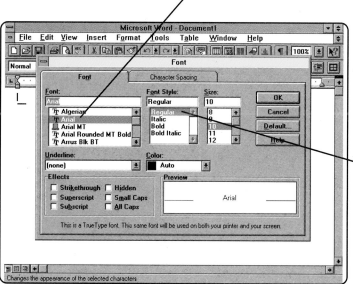

5. Click on **Regular** in the Font Styles list if it is not already highlighted.

Changing the Font Size

Fonts are measured in *points*. Letters are typically written in 10- or 12-point type. In this section you will change the point size of the Arial font from 10 to 12.

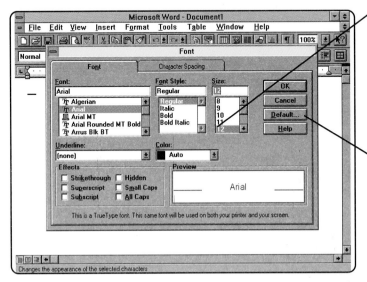

1. Click on 12 to make the font larger.

Changing the Font for Future Documents

1. Click on the **Default button** to set Arial with a point size of 12 as the standard settings for all future documents. (These can, of course, be changed or customized at any time.)

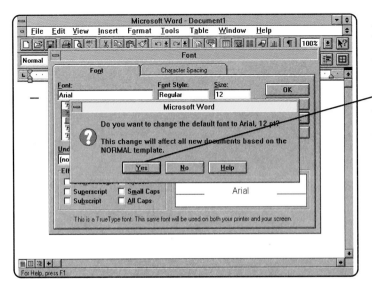

A Microsoft Word message box will appear, asking you to confirm the change.

2. Click on **Yes**. The dialog boxes will close and you will be returned to a screen that looks like the one on the next page.

Notice the font is Arial and the point size is 12.

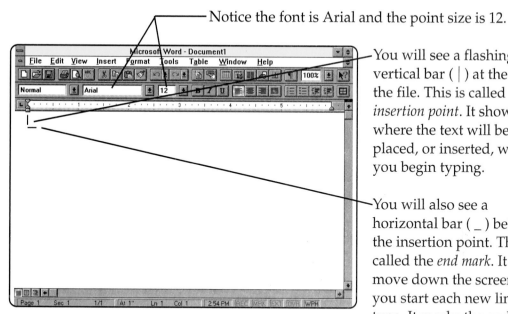

You will see a flashing vertical bar (|) at the top of the file. This is called the *insertion point*. It shows where the text will be placed, or inserted, when you begin typing.

You will also see a horizontal bar (_) below the insertion point. This is called the *end mark*. It will move down the screen as you start each new line of type. It marks the end of the material in the file. Since you haven't entered any text yet, the end mark is at the top of the file.

ENTERING TEXT

You are now ready to type a letter. In the following examples you will type a letter from the Coburn Costume Company inviting a customer to come to the Annual Costume Preview.

The first thing you will type is the company name and return address.

Notice that the insertion point is flashing at the beginning of the document. This means you can start typing and the text will begin at the insertion point.

1. **Press** the **Caps Lock key** to turn on the capital letters feature so that the text you type will appear as capital letters.

2. **Type COBURN COSTUME COMPANY.**

3. **Press Enter.**

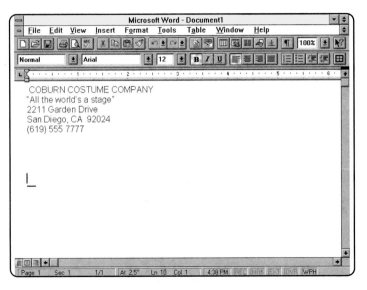

4. **Press** the **Caps Lock key** again to turn off the capital letters feature.

5. **Type "All the world's a stage"** and **press Enter**.

6. **Type 2211 Garden Drive** and **press Enter**.

7. **Type San Diego, CA 92024**. (Press the Spacebar twice after CA.) **Press Enter**.

8. **Type (619) 555-7777.**

9. **Press Enter 5 times**. Your screen will look like this example.

Displaying Paragraph, Space, and Tab Symbols

Word can display symbols for paragraphs, spaces, and tabs. It is helpful to see these symbols when you are setting up a document. Though you can see them on the screen, they will not print.

In this section you will use the Show/Hide ¶ button, to display paragraph, space, and tab symbols.

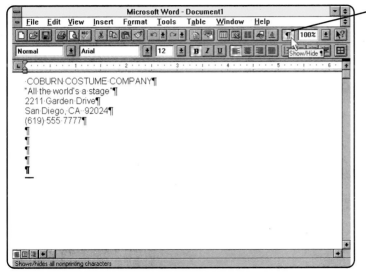

1. Click on the **Show/Hide Paragraph button** (¶) on the right side of the toolbar. When you click on the button it appears pressed in and slightly lighter in color. Paragraph symbols (¶) will now appear in the text.

Notice the dots (·) between the words. Each dot represents a space you create by pressing the Spacebar.

Also notice the ¶ at the end of each line and the five ¶ marks at the end of the text. The ¶ appears each time you press the Enter key.

The Show/Hide Paragraph button works like a toggle switch. Click it once to turn it on. Then click it again to turn it off. Click it a third time to turn it on again. Try it for yourself.

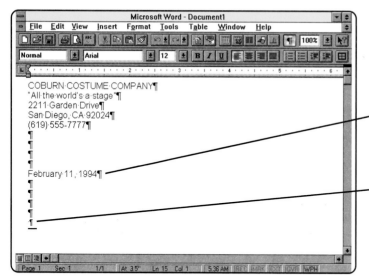

Entering the Date, Address, and Salutation

1. **Type** the **date**. Use today's date instead of the date you see in the example.

2. **Press Enter 5 times**. Five ¶ symbols will appear.

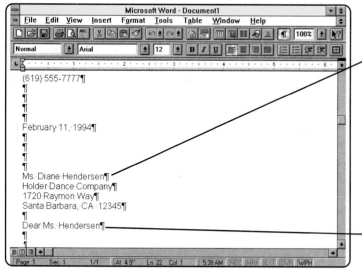

3. **Type** the following lines. **Press Enter** after each line.

Ms. Diane Hendersen
Holder Dance Company
1720 Raymon Way
Santa Barbara, CA 12345
(**Press** the **Spacebar twice** after CA.)

4. **Press Enter twice** after the last line.

5. **Type Dear Ms. Hendersen:** (Don't forget the colon.) The screen will automatically move (scroll) up to make room for the additional lines.

6. **Press Enter twice**.

Entering the Body of the Letter

You are now ready to type the body of the letter. Like all word processing programs, you can continue to type without worrying about your right margin. Word will wrap the text around to the next line automatically. Press the Spacebar only once after the period at the end of a sentence. Press Enter only at the end of a paragraph. Press Enter twice to insert a double line space after a paragraph.

In word processing programs, a paragraph is considered to be any text that is followed by the Enter command. Therefore, each of the single lines you have already typed is considered an individual paragraph.

1. **Type** the text below. It contains errors (shown in red) that you will correct later, so include them if you want to follow along with these procedures. If you make an unintentional typing error, press Backspace and type the correct letters.

We hope you will be her at our Annual Costume Preview on Thursday, March 3, at 2 p.m.

Batman will be here! Mickey Mouse will be here!

Lady Godiva won't be here. (She says she doesn't have a thing to wear.)

Come and see the latest designs for:

Dance Presentations: These include classic ballet costumes, modern, tap, and folk costumes.

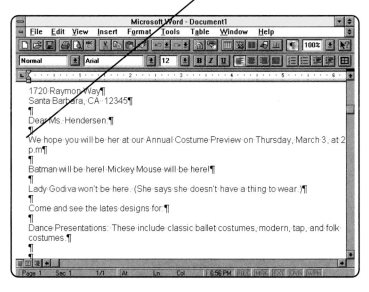

2. **Continue typing** the following text. Remember, press the Enter key *only* at the end of a paragraph.

Theatrical Presentations: These include costumes for performances such as Cats, Les Miserables, and Phantom of the Opera.

Fantasy Costumes: These include childrens and adult's versions of movie characters such as Batman, Catwoman, and Disney characters such as Mickey Mouse.

Historical Characters: These include characters such as Napoleon and Josephine and masks for current political figures.

Because you are a valued customer, Ms. Hendersen, you will recieve a 20 percent discount on any order placed at the Preview.

Please return a copy of the reply form below by Wednesday, February 23.

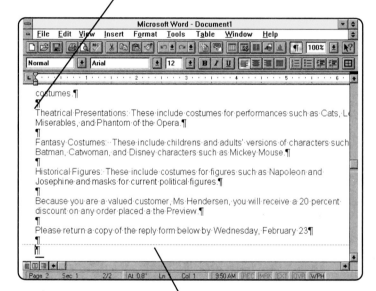

3. **Press Enter twice** after the last line.

Notice the dotted line that appears. This is the *automatic page break*. It indicates the end of the first page. You will change the location of the page break in Chapter 6, "Editing a Document."

The exact location of the automatic page break depends on the margins you set and the size of the font.

Notice the *status bar* at the bottom of your screen.

❶ **Page 2** at the far left of the status bar tells you that the insertion point is on page 2 of the document.

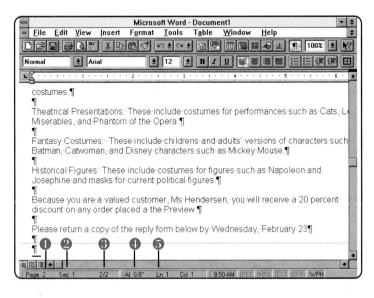

❷ **Sec 1** refers to Word's ability to divide a document into sections. Since you haven't divided the document into sections, the entire document will be labeled "Sec 1."

❸ **2/2** means that you are on page 2 of a 2-page file (document).

❹ **At 0.8"** means that the cursor is 0.8 inch from the top of the page as it will print.

❺ **Ln 1** means that the cursor is on the first line below the top margin. The exact number of lines on the page depends on the width of the margins and the font size you choose.

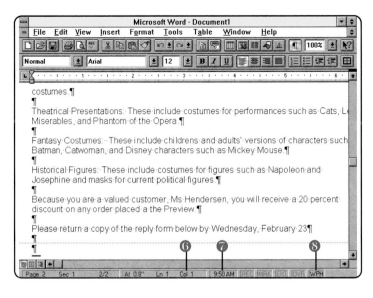

❻ **Col 1** means the cursor is in the first space across the page. The exact number of columns (spaces) that will fit across the page depends on the margins and font size.

❼ This shows you the time.

❽ This is a WordPerfect Help button for previous WordPerfect users.

4. **Type Sincerely,**

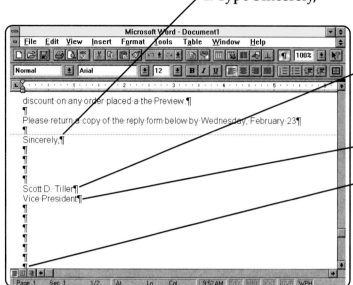

5. **Press Enter four times**.

6. **Type Scott D. Tiller**.

7. **Press Enter**.

8. **Type Vice President**.

9. **Press Enter seven times**. Your screen will look like this example.

INSERTING A SYMBOL AND FINISHING THE LETTER

Windows 3.1 comes with a number of fonts, one of which is called Wingdings. This font has symbols instead of letters. In this section, you will insert a symbols into the text.

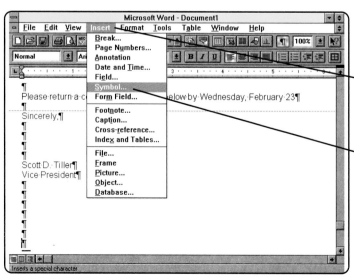

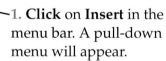

1. **Click** on **Insert** in the menu bar. A pull-down menu will appear.

2. **Click** on **Symbol**. The Symbol dialog box will appear.

3. **Click** on ⬇ to the right of the Symbols Font box. A drop-down list of fonts will appear. The contents of the list depends on the fonts you have installed on your computer. Your list may be different from the one you see in this example.

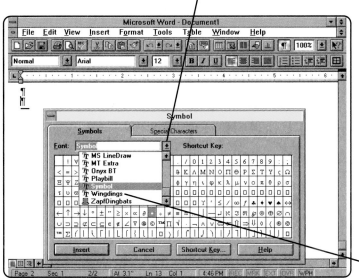

4. **Click** on ⬆ or ⬇ to scroll up or down the list until you see Wingdings. (It's possible that Wingdings already shows in the box.)

5. **Click** on **Wingdings**. The drop-down list will disappear and Wingdings will appear in the Symbols Font box. The Wingdings symbol set will appear on the screen.

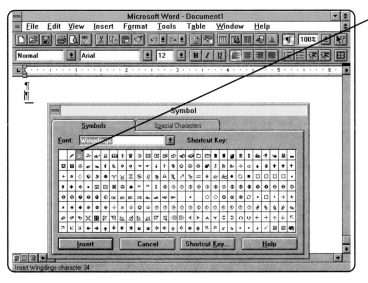

6. **Place** the mouse pointer on the scissors symbol, which is in the third position from the left in the first row. (It's possible that your scissors may be in a different spot.)

7. Click the **left mouse button** to select the scissors. The symbol will be enlarged so you can see it better.

You can repeat steps 6 through 8 to see other symbols. Make sure to click on the scissors again when you have finished.

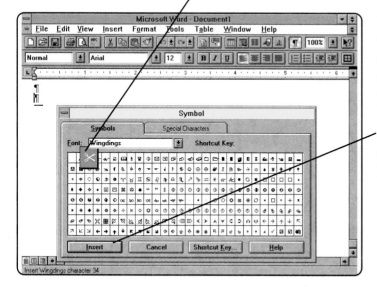

8. Click on **Insert**. The scissors will appear in the letter at the insertion point.

9. Click on **Close**. The Symbol dialog box will close.

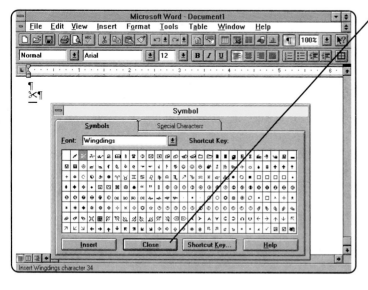

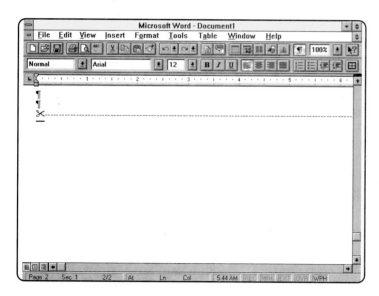

10. Press and hold the **Hyphen key** (-) until the hyphens go all the way across the page. If you go too far, the extra hyphens will wrap around to the next line. Simply press the Backspace key until the insertion point goes back to the previous line.

11. Press Enter twice.

12. Type the sentence **I will be attending.** Then **press Enter twice**.

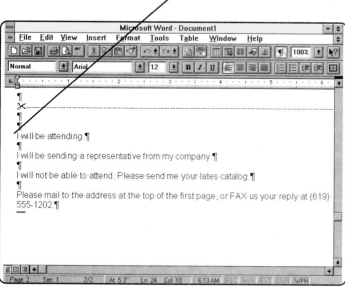

13. Type the sentence **I will be sending a representative from my company.** Then **press Enter twice**.

14. Type the following sentences : **I will not be able to attend. Please send me your latest catalog.** Then, **press Enter twice.**

15. Type the sentence **Please mail to the address at the top of the first page, or FAX us your reply at (619) 555-1202.**

Congratulations! You just typed your first letter in Word. In Chapter 2, you will name the letter and save it.

Naming and Saving a Document

Saving a file is as easy as clicking your mouse in Word for Windows 6. There's even an Automatic Save feature that you can use to save your work at specific intervals. Word is set up to save files to the winword6 directory. In this chapter you will do the following:

❖ Name and save a document

❖ Set the Automatic Save feature to save your document every 10 minutes

NAMING AND SAVING A FILE

In this section you will name the letter you typed in Chapter 1 and save it.

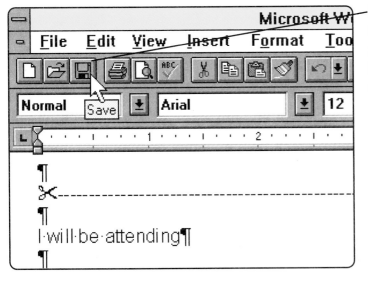

1. **Click** on the **Save Tool** in the toolbar. Since you have not named the file yet, the Save As dialog box will appear.

Notice the open folders beside c:\ and winword6. These tell you that you are currently working in the winword6 directory on the C drive. This is where your file will be saved.

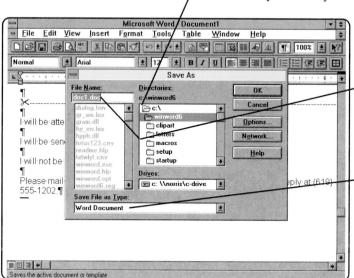

2. Type preview. It will replace the highlighted doc1.doc that is in the File Name box.

3. Confirm that **Word Document** is in the Save File as Type box. This means that the file will be saved as a Word document file.

SAVING AUTOMATICALLY

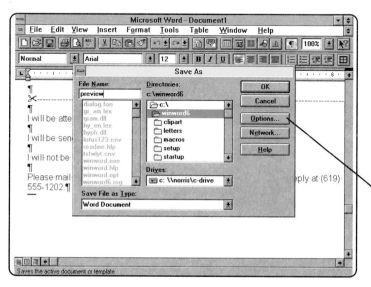

You can set Word to save your work automatically at specific intervals. This does not take the place of a Save command, but it provides a handy backup in case of a power outage or system failure.

1 Click on **Options**.

2. **Click** on the **Save Tab** if it is not in the front.

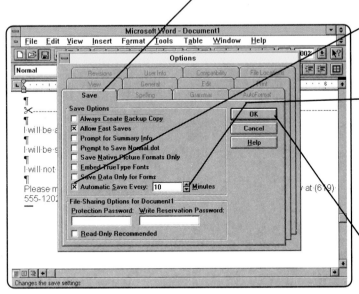

3. **Click** on the box next to **Automatic Save** to insert an × if one is not already there.

4. **Click** the ▲ to increase the time between automatic saves. **Click** the ▼ to decrease the time between automatic saves. In this example, the time will be left at 10 minutes.

5. **Click** on **OK**. The Options dialog box will close.

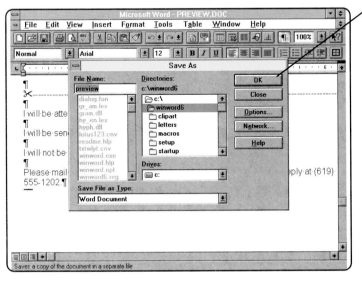

6. **Click** on **OK**. The Save As dialog box will disappear and the letter will be saved.

Notice that the filename, PREVIEW.DOC, is now shown in the title bar instead of Document1.

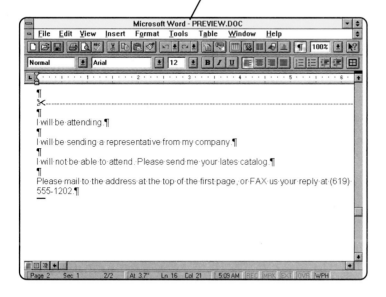

Previewing and Printing a Document

There are several ways to print a document in Word 6. You can print the whole document, the current page, or selected pages. But before you actually print a file, you can take advantage of the Print Preview feature to see how the document will look on the printed page. In this chapter you will do the following:

❖ Preview a document before printing it

❖ Print a document

VIEWING A DOCUMENT BEFORE PRINTING

In this section you will use the Print Preview button on the toolbar to view a document before printing. If you don't have the PREVIEW.DOC file open, open it now. If you have been following along with the previous examples, you should be at the end of the file on page 2. If your cursor is not at this location, press and hold the Ctrl key and then press the End key (Ctrl + End) to go to the end of the file.

1. **Click** on the **Print Preview button**. The Print Preview screen will appear showing you the page on which your cursor is located.

Magnifying the View in Print Preview

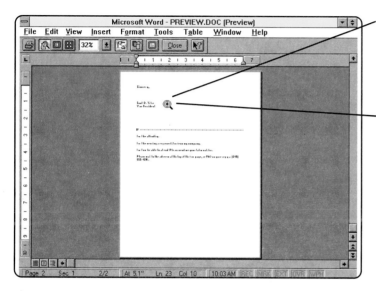

Notice that your mouse pointer is in the shape of a magnifying glass with a little + sign in it.

1. **Click once** with your left mouse button. A magnified view of page 2 will appear on your screen.

Notice that instead of the + inside the magnifying glass there is now a - sign.

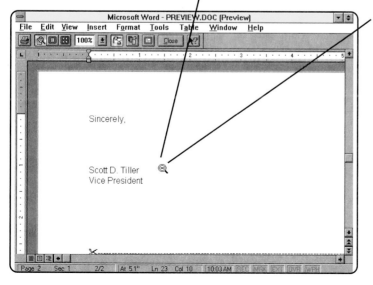

2. **Click once** to zoom out to a full page view again.

Viewing Multiple Pages in Print Preview

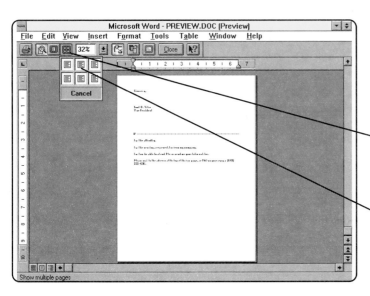

So far you have seen only one page in Print Preview. With the Multiple Pages button you can see up to six pages at one time.

1. **Click** on the **Multiple Pages button**. A menu will appear.

2. **Click** on the **second page**. This will display two pages of the document. (You can display up to six pages.)

Changing Pages in Preview

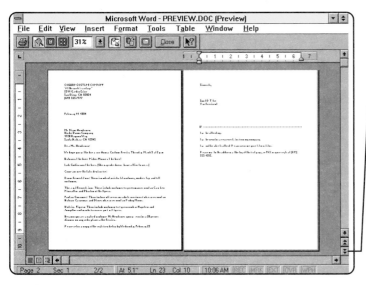

Notice the border around page 2. This is the page where your cursor is located.

If you had more than two pages in your document, you would click on the double arrow at the bottom of the scroll bar. This would display pages 2 and 3.

PRINTING WITH THE PRINT BUTTON

In this section you will use the Print button to print the entire file with a click of your mouse.

1. Click on the **Print button**. The Printing message box will appear.

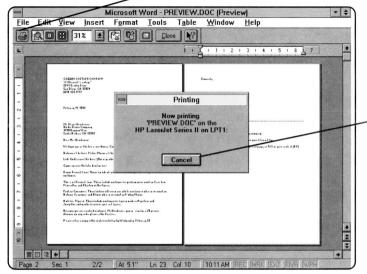

The Printing message box updates you as it prints each page of your document.

Notice that you can stop the printing by clicking on Cancel. You must wait until the Printing message box disappears before you can continue to work.

Closing Print Preview

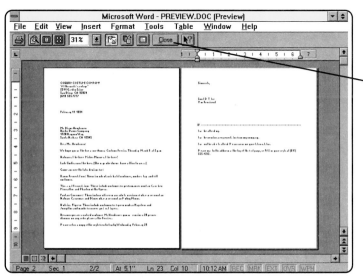

1. Click on **Close** to close Print Preview. You will return to the Normal View screen.

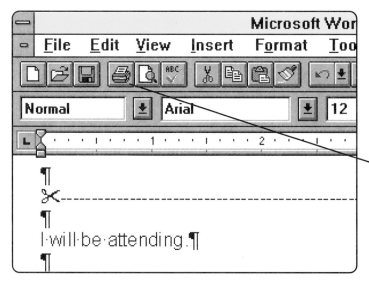

PRINTING FROM THE MENU BAR

In this section you will use the Print command on the File pull-down menu.

Notice that you can use the Print button on the standard toolbar to print the entire file at the click of your mouse.

1. Click on **File** in the menu bar. A pull-down menu will appear.

2. Click on **Print**. The Print dialog box will appear.

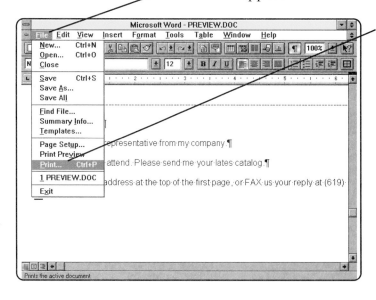

Printing Selected Pages

In this section you will not actually make any of the following changes in the Print dialog box, but you should be aware of the options available to you.

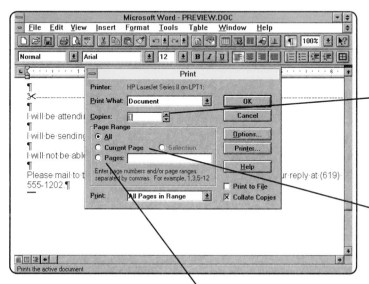

Notice that you can change the number of copies you want to print by clicking on the up arrow in the Copies box.

Notice that you can print only the page where the cursor is located by clicking on Current Page.

Notice that you can print specific pages by typing page numbers separated by commas. You can also type a range of pages. For example 1-4,7,9,17-20.

Notice that there is an X in the box beside Collate Copies. This means that multiple copies will be automatically collated (put in order) as they print.

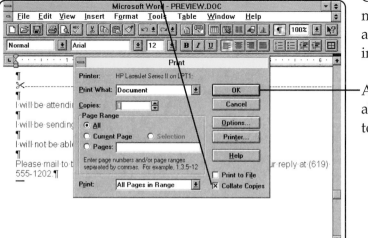

After you make any of the above changes, **click** on **OK** to print.

Printing the Entire Document

In this section you will print all of the pages in the document.

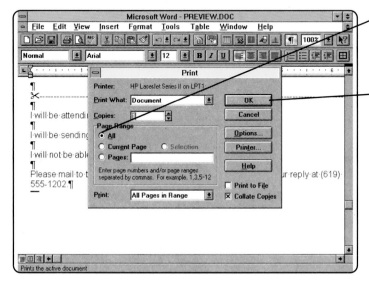

1. **Click** on **All** to insert a dot in the circle if one is not already there.

2. **Click** on **OK**. You will see the Printing message box that you saw when you used the Print button.

Closing a File and Opening a Saved File

Because Word for Windows 6 is a Windows-based program, it uses standard Windows commands to open and close files. As in all Windows programs, there are several ways to open and close files. In this chapter you will do the following:

❖ Close a file

❖ Close Word for Windows

❖ Learn two ways to open a saved file

SAVING AND CLOSING A FILE

In this section you will close the PREVIEW.DOC file you created in Chapter 1. Even though you saved the file in Chapter 2, these procedures will start with saving the file. Saving often is a good habit to develop.

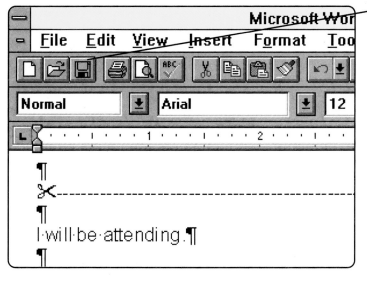

1. Click on the **Save button** in the toolbar.

The hourglass will appear briefly along with a series of dashes in your status bar to indicate the percent of the file saved. You won't see any other difference in your screen, but the file and any changes are now saved. Since you already saved the file, you will not see the Save As dialog box.

Closing a File

1. Click on **File** in the menu bar. A pull-down menu will appear.

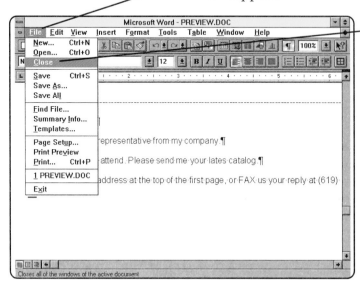

2. Click on **Close**. The file will close and you will see a blank Word screen.

CLOSING WORD FOR WINDOWS

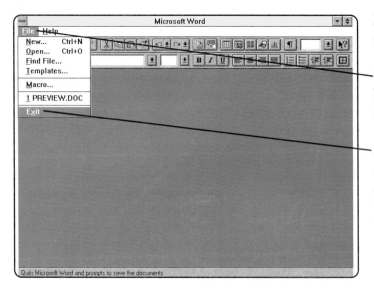

In this section you will close the Word program.

1. Click on **File** in the menu bar. A pull-down menu will appear.

2. Click on **Exit**. Word will close and you will be back at Program Manager with the group that contains Word.

BOOTING UP WORD

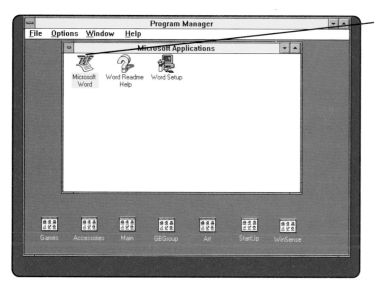

1. Click twice on the **Microsoft Word icon**.

After a pause, Word will appear on your screen with a blank Document1 file.

The Tip of the Day dialog box will appear on your screen unless you have turned this feature off as shown in Chapter 1.

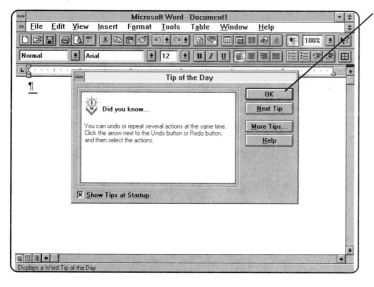

2. Click on **OK** to close the Tip of the Day dialog box.

OPENING A SAVED FILE

There are several ways to open a saved file. In Method #1, you will use the File pull-down menu.

Method #1

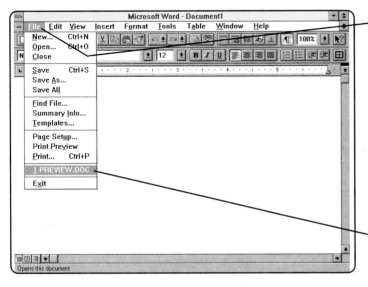

1. **Click** on **File** in the menu bar. A pull-down menu will appear.

The File pull-down menu lists the four most recent files you have opened. If you have a new Word 6, there will be only one file listed. If others have used Word before you, you may see up to four files listed.

2. **Click** on **PREVIEW.DOC** in the file list. The file will appear on your screen.

Method #2

Method #2 uses the Open tool in the toolbar. In order to try this method, you will close PREVIEW.DOC.

1. **Click twice** on the **Control Menu box** (⊟) to the left of the menu bar. (Be careful not to click on the Control Menu box in the Microsoft Word title bar. That will close the entire program.) The file will close and you will see a blank Word screen.

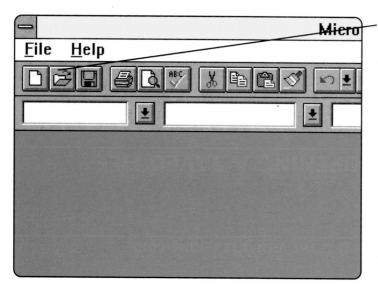

2. **Click** on the **Open tool** in the toolbar. The Open dialog box will appear.

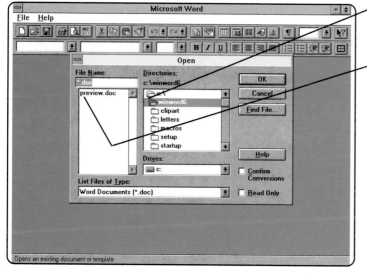

Notice that the WINWORD6 folder is open.

3. **Click twice** on **preview.doc** in the File Name list box. (You can also click once on preview.doc to highlight it, then click on OK.) The file will appear on your screen.

In the next chapter you will learn how to use the Grammar and Spelling Checker and the Thesaurus that come with Word.

Using the Grammar and Spelling Checker, and Thesaurus

Word will check your grammar and spelling and make suggestions for changes. Word also contains a Thesaurus that will offer a list of word substitutes. Now, if it would only go out for coffee . . .

In this chapter you will do the following:

❖ Use the Grammar and Spelling Checker

❖ Use the Thesaurus

USING THE GRAMMAR AND SPELL CHECKER

You can use the Spelling Check independently. When you use the Grammar Check, however, the Spelling Check is included. This example shows the cursor at the top of the PREVIEW.DOC file.

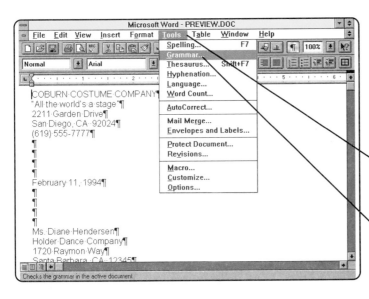

1. **Press and hold** the **Ctrl key** as you **press** the **Home key** (Ctrl + Home). This will move the cursor to the beginning of the file.

2. **Click** on **Tools** in the menu bar. A pull-down menu will appear.

3. **Click** on **Grammar**. A dialog box will appear.

Notice that COBURN is highlighted in the letter and the Spelling dialog box is on your screen.

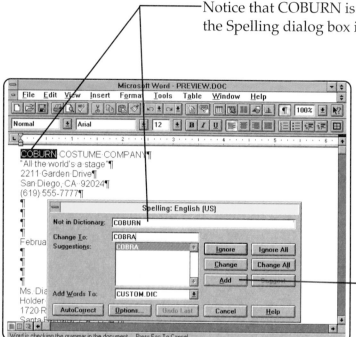

Adding a Word to the Dictionary

Since the company name will be used constantly in your communications, add it to the Custom dictionary. This means that Word will recognize the name in the future and not tag it as a misspelled or unrecognized word.

1. Click on **Add.** You will see an hourglass as Word goes to the next misspelled word or grammar error.

Ignoring a Suggested Change

The dictionary is not programmed to recognize most

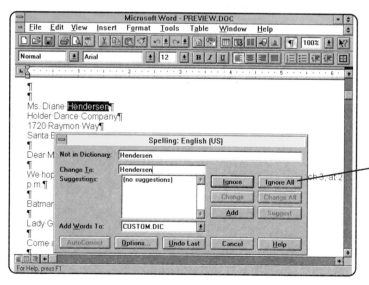

proper names. If the name is one which you will use often, add it to the dictionary as you did above. If you will not use it often, you can choose to ignore Word's identification of it as a misspelled word.

1. Click on **Ignore All.** Because Hendersen appears more than once in the letter, this will tell Word to ignore all occurrences of it.

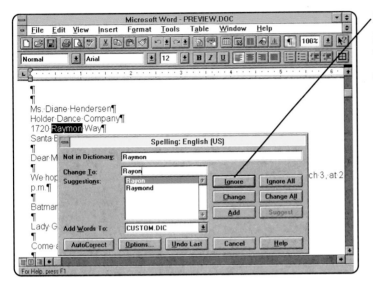

2. **Click** on **Ignore** because Raymon is spelled correctly. Word will go to the next spelling or grammar error.

Making a Correction in the Letter

Sometimes Word will point out a change that you must make yourself, as in the time change in this example.

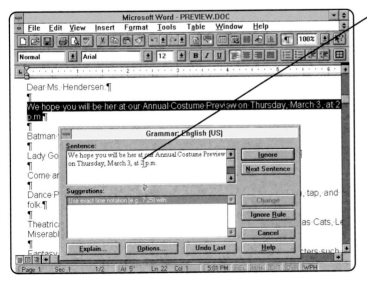

1. **Place** the mouse pointer to the **right of 2** in the dialog box. The pointer will be in the shape of an I-beam.

2. **Click** to set the cursor in place.

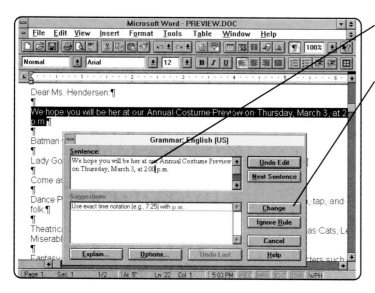

3. Type :00. The time now is 2:00.

4. Click on **Change** to make the change in the letter and resume the Grammar and Spelling check.

Continuing the Grammar and Spelling Check

Notice the Spelling dialog box has appeared on top of the Grammar dialog box.

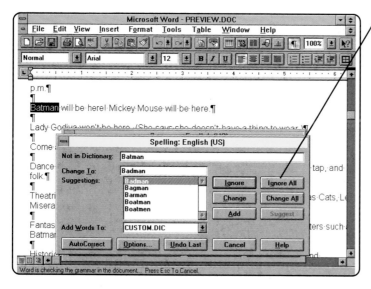

1. Click on **Ignore All** when Word identifies Batman as an unrecognized word.

2. Click on **Ignore** when Word identifies Godiva as a misspelled word.

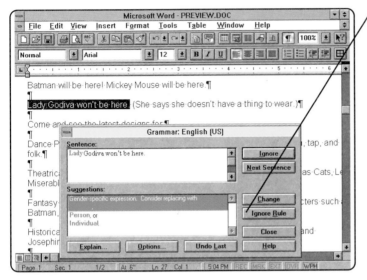

3. **Click** on **Ignore Rule** because the rule does not apply to this example.

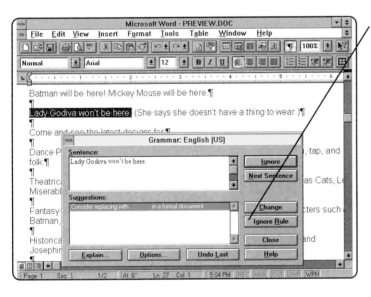

4. **Click** on **Ignore Rule** to ignore the suggestion to make the expression more formal.

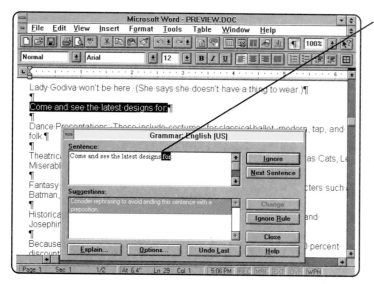

5. Click to the **right** of **designs** to place the cursor.

6. Press and hold the **mouse button** and **drag** the highlight bar over the space after designs and the word "for." Be careful not to highlight the colon.

7. Press the **Backspace key** on your keyboard to delete the highlighted text.

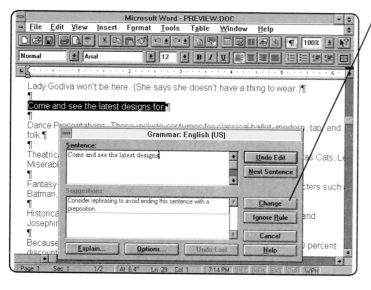

8. Click on **Change** to make the change in the letter and to continue the Grammar and Spelling Check.

9. Click on **Ignore** when Word identifies the following as misspelled words:

❖ **Les**

❖ **Miserables**

Correcting a Spelling Error

When Spelling Check identifies a misspelled word, it suggests a list of possible changes.

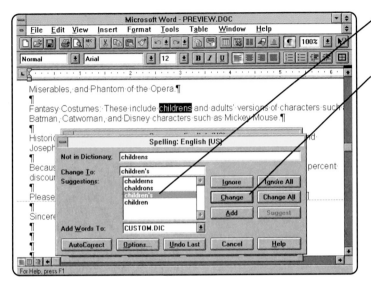

1. **Click** on **children's** to highlight it.

2. **Click** on **Change**. Word will correct the error and move to the next error.

3. **Click** on **Ignore** when Word identifies Catwoman as a misspelled word.

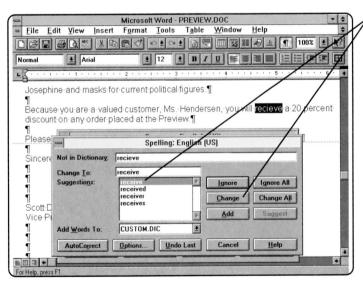

4. Because the correct spelling of receive is already highlighted in the Suggestions list, **click** on **Change.**

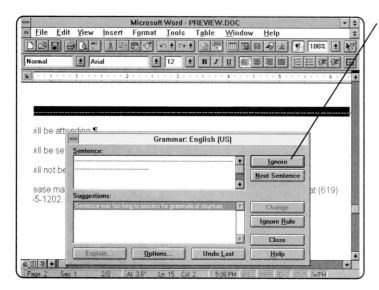

5. Click on **Ignore** when Word identifies the hyphens as an error.

When the grammar check is complete, Word displays statistics about the readability of the document. See the *Microsoft Word for Windows User's Guide* for more information about the readability of the document.

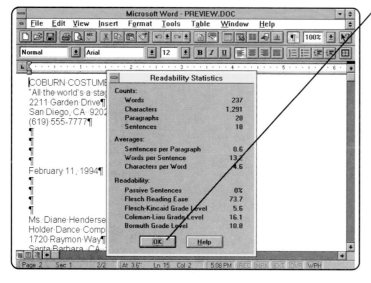

6. Click on **OK**. The dialog box will disappear and you will be returned to the beginning of the letter.

Although this example showed the Grammar and Spelling Check beginning from the top of the file, you can begin the Grammar and Spelling Check anywhere. It will start at your cursor, go to the end of the file, then wrap around to the undone section at the beginning of the file.

USING THE THESAURUS

In this section you will use the Thesaurus to see words that can replace "latest." First, however, you will use the Find command to locate the word.

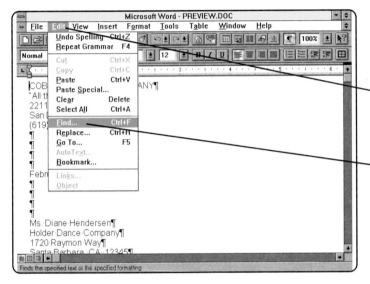

Using the Find Command

1. Click on **Edit** in the menu bar. A pull-down menu will appear.

2. Click on **Find**. The Find dialog box will appear.

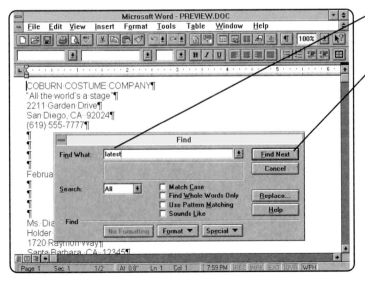

3. Type the word **latest** in the Find What box.

4. Click on **Find Next**. Because you are at the top of the file, Word will highlight the first occurrence of "latest" in the letter.

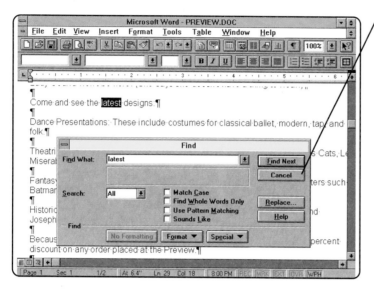

5. Click on **Cancel** to close the Find dialog box.

Using the Thesaurus

Normally you must highlight the word you want to check with the Thesaurus. If you have been following these procedures, "latest" was highlighted by the Find command. Therefore, you can simply continue with the following steps.

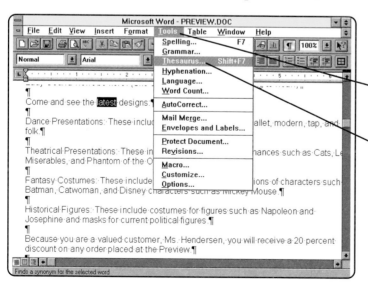

1. Click on **Tools**. A pull-down menu will appear.

2. Click on **Thesaurus**. The Thesaurus dialog box will appear.

3. **Click** on **newest** in the Synonyms list box. It will be highlighted.

4. **Click** on **Replace** to make the change.

5. **Click** on the ⬆ on the scroll bar to scroll up to the first sentence in the letter.

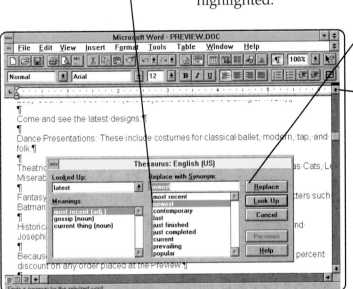

Notice that Word did not identify "her" in the first sentence as a misspelled word. This is because "her" is a word. It is incorrectly spelled only in the context of this sentence. Computers are not ready to take over the world just yet...

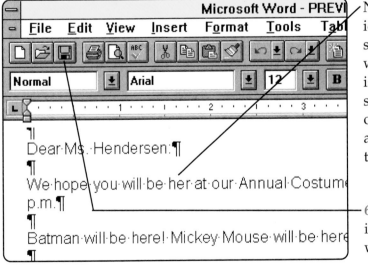

6. **Click** on the **Save button** in the toolbar to save your work.

In Chapter 6, "Editing a Document," you will correct this error and make other changes in the letter.

Editing a Document

If this is the first time you have used a Windows-based word processing program, you will be delighted with the ease with which you can edit a document. Word 6 for Windows has even improved on standard Windows editing commands by adding special features such as drag-and-drop moving and Edit Undo. In this chapter you will do the following:

❖ Add and delete letters and words and combine paragraphs

❖ Use the Edit Undo feature

❖ Use the Replace All command to correct an error that occurs in several places

❖ Move and copy text

❖ Insert and change the position of the page break

ADDING LETTERS AND WORDS

In this section you will make a number of corrections to the letter. The first will be to change "her" to "here."

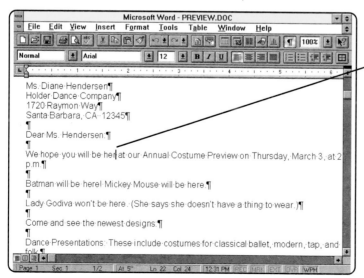

1. **Place** the mouse pointer at the **end** of **"her."** Notice that the mouse pointer is in the shape of an I-beam when it is in the letter. **Click** to set it in place.

2. **Type** the letter **e**. The word will become "here." Notice that "2:00" moves to the next line automatically.

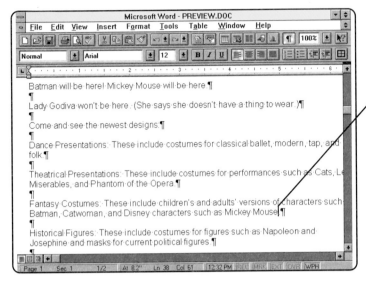

3. Click on ⬇ on the scroll bar to scroll until you can see two lines beginning with "Fantasy Costumes."

4. Place the mouse pointer at the end of the sentence **between "Mouse" and the period. Click** the mouse button to set the insertion point in place.

5. Press the **Spacebar** then **type** the words **and Donald Duck.** Notice that the period moves as you add words.

DELETING AND REPLACING WORDS AND COMBINING PARAGRAPHS

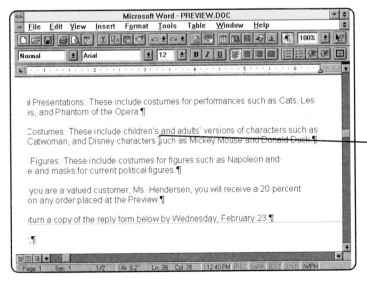

In this section, you will delete unnecessary words.

Deleting Words

1. Place the I-beam at the left of **"such as."** Be careful not to highlight the space (.) before such as or you will delete the space between the words.

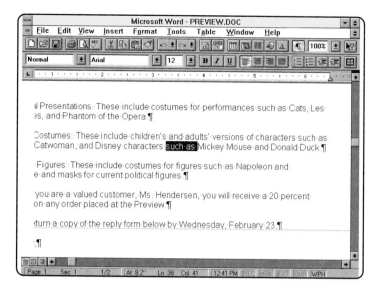

2. Press and hold the mouse button and **drag** the mouse pointer **over "such as"** and the **space after** as. They will be highlighted.

3. Release the mouse button, then **press** the **Backspace key** on your keyboard. The highlighted words will disappear.

Undoing an Edit

What if you decide you don't want to delete those words? Word has an Undo feature that makes it easy for you to change your mind as long as you haven't done anything else after deleting the words.

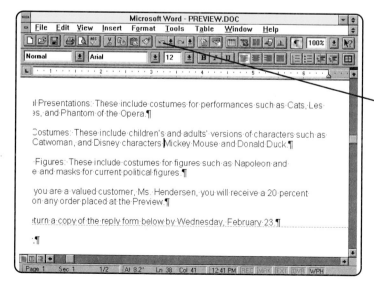

1. Click on the **Undo button** in the toolbar. The deleted words will be restored to the text.

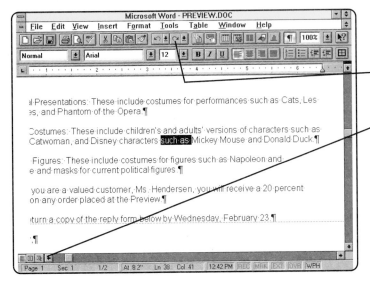

To undo the undo is just as easy.

2. Click on the **Redo button** in the toolbar.

3. Click on ◄ on the bottom scroll bar to move the screen view back to the left margin.

Combining Paragraphs

In this section you will put the Lady Godiva sentences into the preceding paragraph with Batman and Mickey Mouse.

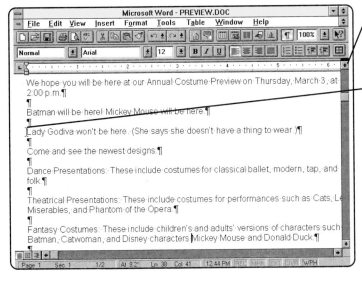

1. Click on ▲ to scroll up to the sentence beginning with "Lady Godiva."

2. Place the mouse pointer at the **beginning** of the **"Lady Godiva"** sentence. Make sure the pointer is in the shape of an I-beam. Place the pointer as close to "Lady" as you can to ensure that it is an I-beam. **Click** to set it in place.

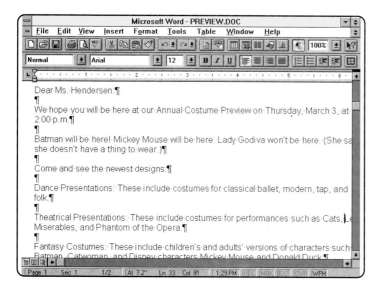

3. Press the **Backspace key twice** then **press** the **Spacebar.** This will bring the entire Lady Godiva paragraph up to the end of the Mickey Mouse sentence and put a space between the sentences.

INSERTING A SOFT RETURN

In the example you see here, it would look better if "Les" was on the same line with "Miserables." If you press the Enter key, however, you will insert a paragraph mark (called a *hard return*) and make the second line a separate paragraph. You can, however, move "Les" to the next line with what is called a *soft return*. Unlike hard returns, soft returns are not recognized as paragraph endings in Word. This is an important formatting distinction, which will be discussed in Chapter 7, "Customizing Text."

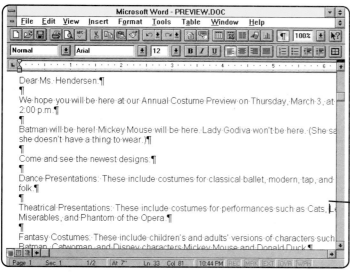

1. Place the mouse pointer to the **left** of **"Les,"** after the dot. **Click** to set it in place.

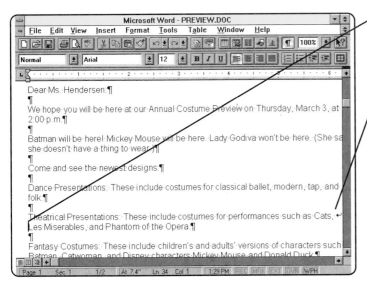

2. Press and hold the **Shift key** as you **press Enter** (Shift + Enter). "Les" will move to the next line.

Notice the symbol indicating a soft return at the end of the line.

3. Press and hold the **Ctrl key** as you **press End** (Ctrl + End). This will take you to the end of the file.

INSERTING A HARD RETURN

In this example, you will not use the soft return. Instead you will use a hard return to change the spacing in the very last line of the letter.

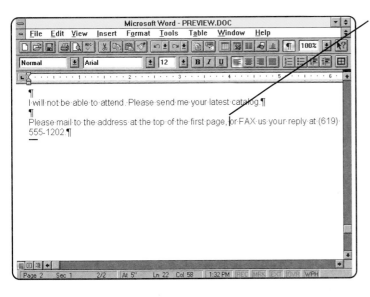

1. Click to the **left** of **"or"** in the last line of the letter.

2. Press Enter. This will move the cursor and the following text to the next line. These will now be two separate paragraphs.

USING THE REPLACE COMMAND

In this example you will replace "sen" at the end of "Hendersen" with "son." You can replace each "sen" individually or you can use the Replace command to find and replace each occurrence automatically. You will start tat the top of the file since the Replace command begins at the cursor and goes to the end of the file.

1. Press and hold the **Ctrl key** as you **press** the **Home key** (Ctrl + Home) to go to the beginning of your file.

2. Click on **Edit** in the menu bar. A pull-down menu will appear.

3. Click on **Replace**. The Replace dialog box will appear. The cursor will be flashing in the Find What box.

4. Type Hendersen.

5. Click on the **Replace With box** and **type Henderson**.

6. Click on **Replace All**. An hourglass will appear briefly as Word makes all the changes. (See the *User's Guide* for more details about the Replace command.)

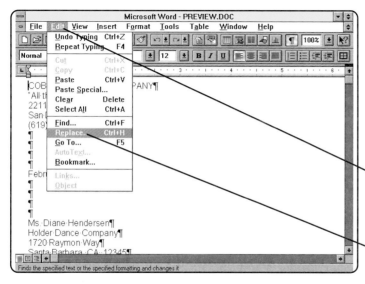

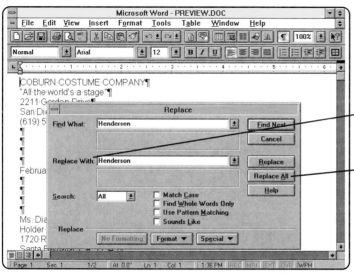

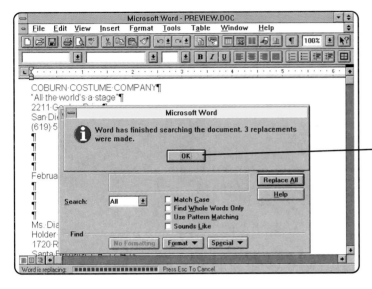

When Word is finished replacing the text, a Microsoft Word message box will appear telling you how many replacements were made.

7. **Click** on **OK** to close the message box. You will see the Replace dialog box.

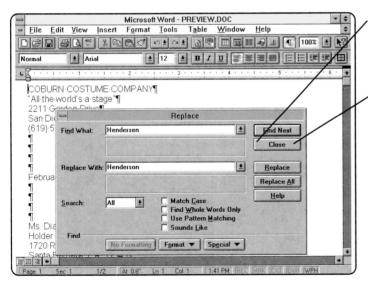

Notice that the Cancel button in the Replace dialog box has changed to Close.

8. **Click** on **Close**. The dialog box will disappear and the letter will be on your screen with all the corrections made. Pretty neat, don't you think?

DRAG-AND-DROP MOVING

In this section you will move the first sentence to a different spot in the letter.

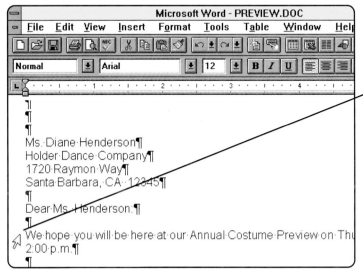

1. Click on ⬇ to scroll down so that you can see the first three or four paragraphs.

2. Place the **mouse pointer** in the left margin **beside the first paragraph**.

3. Click twice. The entire paragraph will be highlighted. (If you click once only the single line beside the arrow will be highlighted.)

4. Place the mouse pointer **on top of "We."**

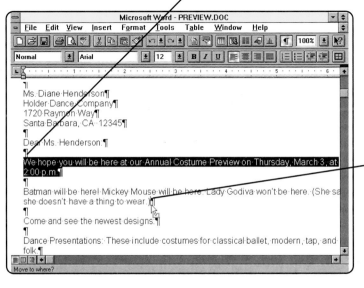

5. Press and hold the mouse button and **drag** the pointer down to the **end of the next paragraph**. You will see a dotted insertion point and a small square being dragged by the arrow.

6. Place the dotted insertion point to the **left of the paragraph symbol** and **release** the mouse button. The paragraph will be moved to that spot.

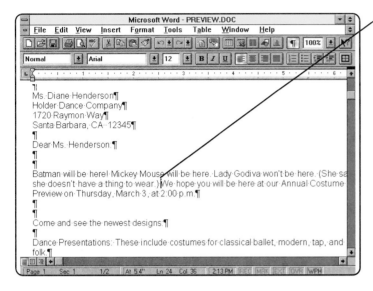

7. Click to the **left** of **"We hope."** The highlighting will disappear and you will see the flashing insertion point.

8. Press Enter twice to insert a double space between the end of the Batman paragraph and the We hope paragraph.

Notice that there is now an extra paragraph mark (and a blank line) at the beginning of the letter.

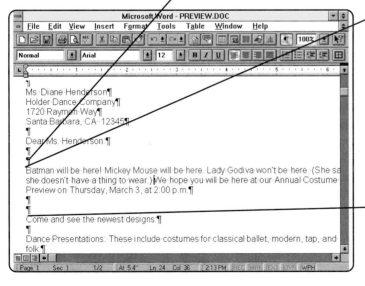

9. Place the mouse pointer at the **beginning of the "Batman" sentence**. Click to set it in place.

10. Press the **Backspace key once**. The sentence is moved up one line and the blank line is removed.

11. Repeat steps 9 and 10 to remove the blank line above the "Come and see" sentence.

INSERTING A PAGE BREAK

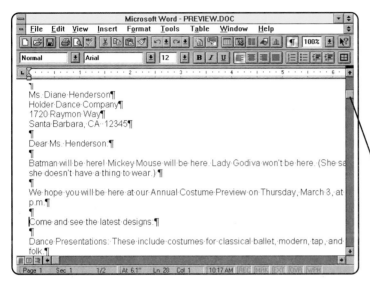

Word does not necessarily insert an automatic page break in a place that makes sense within the context of the document. Fortunately, it's easy to change the position of the page break.

1. **Click and hold** on the **scroll button** and **drag** it half way down the scroll bar. This will bring you half way through the document and you will be able to see the automatic page break.

2. **Click** to the **left** of the **"Please return"** sentence.

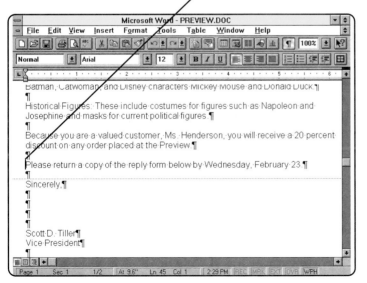

3. **Press and hold** the **Ctrl key** as you **press Enter**. A page break will be inserted into the letter at the insertion point.

When you insert a page break into text, the automatic page break disappears.

Changing the Position of a Page Break

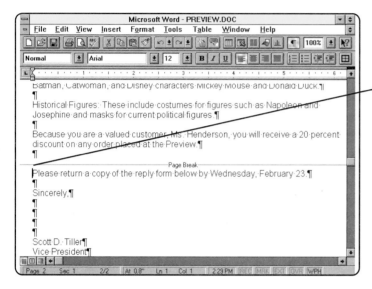

In this example you will delete the page break you just inserted.

1. Click to the **left** of the **first sentence after** the **page break**. If you have been following along, your cursor is already there.

2. Press the **Backspace key**. The page break will be deleted and the automatic page break will appear again.

3. Click on the **Undo button** to reinsert the permanent page break.

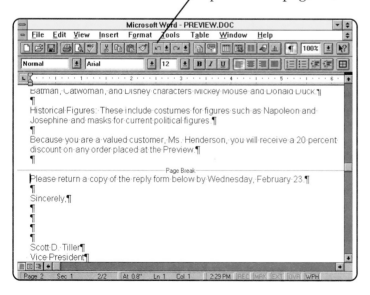

COPYING AND PASTING TEXT

In this section you will learn two ways to copy text from one section of a document to another.

Copying and Pasting Text with the Edit Menu

In this example you will copy text from page 1 of the letter onto page 2.

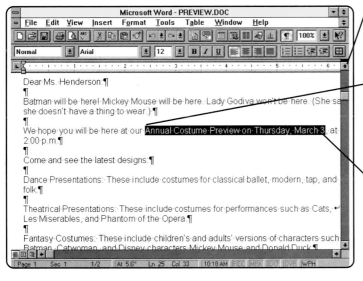

1. Click on ⬆ to scroll up so you can see the salutation on page 1.

2. Place the mouse pointer to the **left** of **"Annual Costume Preview." Click** to set it in place.

3. Press and hold the mouse button and **drag** the insertion point **over** "**Annual Costume Preview on Thursday, March 3."** They will be highlighted.

4. Release the mouse button.

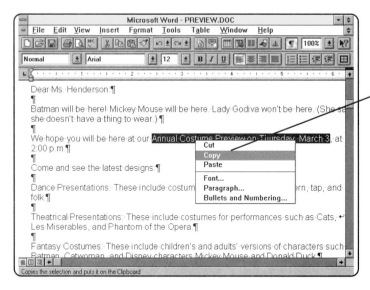

5. Click you **right mouse button**. A quick menu will appear.

6. Click on **Copy**. You will not see any change in your screen, but the highlighted text is now copied to the Clipboard. It will stay there until it is replaced by text from another Copy, Cut, or Delete command.

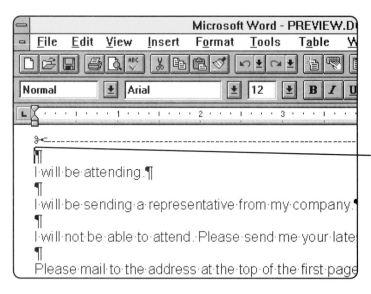

7. Press and hold the **Ctrl key**, then **press** the **End key** (Ctrl + End).

8. Click on ⬆ until you can see the scissors.

9. Place the mouse pointer to the **left** of the **paragraph symbol** just below the scissors. **Click** to set the pointer in place.

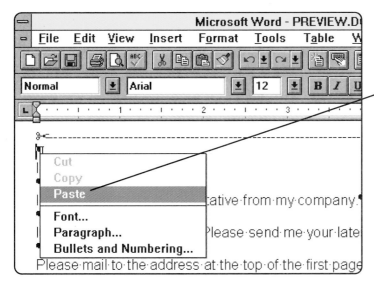

10. **Click** on your **right mouse button**. A quick menu will appear.

11. **Click** on **Paste**. The text that you copied to the Clipboard will be copied into the document starting at the insertion point.

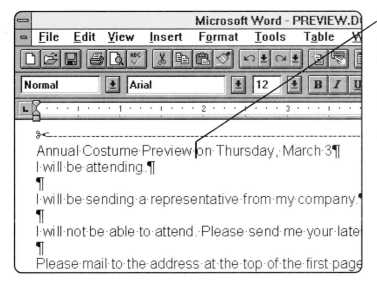

12. **Place** the mouse pointer to the **left** of **"on."** Click to set it in place.

13. **Press Enter** to move "on Thursday, March 3" to the next line.

14. **Place** the mouse pointer to the **left** of **"on."** If you place it close to the word it will change to an I-beam. You may have to fiddle with the position of the pointer to get it to change to the I-beam. (If you place it too far out in the left margin it will change to an arrow and the arrow won't perform the following procedure.)

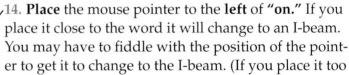
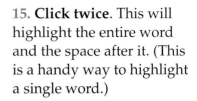
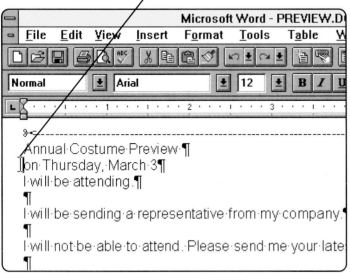

15. **Click twice**. This will highlight the entire word and the space after it. (This is a handy way to highlight a single word.)

16. **Press** the **Backspace key**. The highlighted text will be deleted.

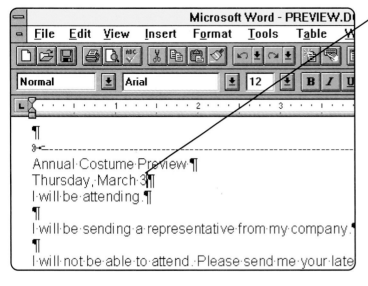

17. **Place** the mouse pointer to the **left** of the paragraph symbol at the **end** of **"March 3." Click** to set it in place.

18. **Press Enter twice** to insert two blank lines after the date.

Using the Copy Button

In this three-part example you will use the Copy and Paste tools to copy Ms. Henderson's name and address on the first page and place it on the return form on the second page. First you will copy the text.

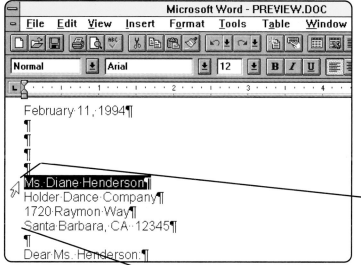

1. Press and hold the **Ctrl key**, then **press** the **Home key** (Ctrl + Home) to go to the top of the file. Then scroll down until you can see Ms. Henderson's name and address.

2. Click in the left margin **beside "Ms. Diane Henderson."** The line will be highlighted.

3. Press and hold the **Shift key** and **click** in the left margin **next to the last line of the address**. All lines between the first and second clicks will be highlighted. (This is a quick way to select a series of paragraphs.)

4. Click on the **Copy button** in the toolbar.

In the next procedure, you will use the Go To command to get to page 2 quickly.

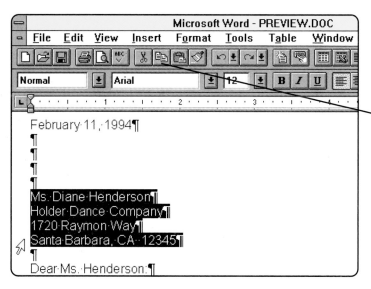

Using the Go To Command

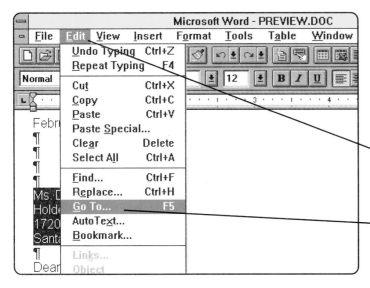

Using the Go To command is a quick way to move around in multipage documents. In this example you will use it to go to the top of page 2.

1. Click on **Edit** in the menu bar. A pull-down menu will appear.

2. Click on **Go To**. The Go To dialog box will appear.

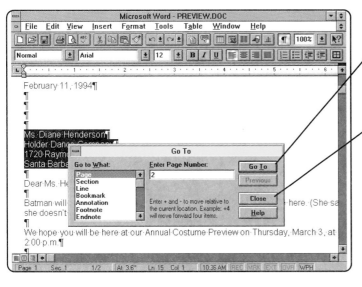

3. Type the **number 2**.

4. Click on **Go To**. The insertion point will move to the top of page 2.

5. Click on **Close**. The Go To box will disappear and page 2 will be displayed on your screen.

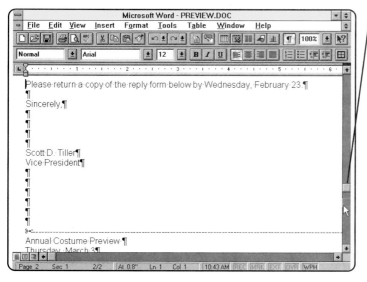

6. Click on the **scroll bar** about three quarters of the way down. This will take you three quarters of the way through the file and bring the return form into view.

Using the Paste Tool

1. Place the mouse pointer to the **left** of the **paragraph symbol above "I will be attending." Click** to set the cursor in place.

2. Press Enter to insert another blank line in the text. You will now see three paragraph symbols above the sentence "I will be attending.".

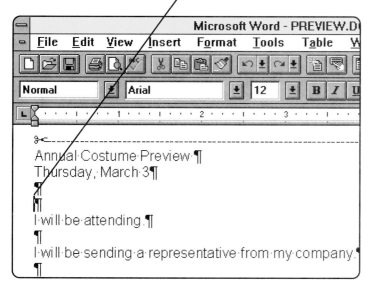

3. **Click** on the **Paste button** in the toolbar.

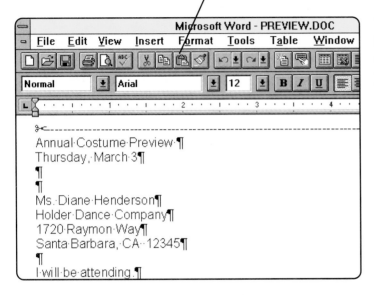

The text you copied to the Clipboard with the Copy tool is now pasted in the letter at the insertion point.

4. **Click** on the **Save button** in the toolbar to save your work.

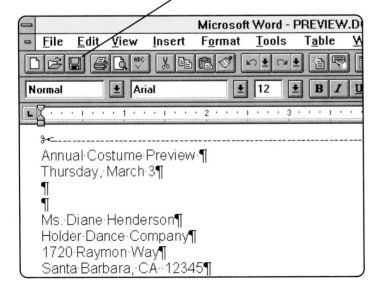

Program Manager ▼ ▲

Part II   Formatting a Document ▼ ▲

Customizing Text

You will love the ease with which you can add special features to your text, such as bold and italic type. You can further emphasize portions of the text by changing the size of the font. You can center text and create a bulleted list at the click of your mouse. In this chapter you will do the following:

❖ Change type size

❖ Make text **bold**, *italic*, and <u>underlined</u>

❖ Center text

❖ Make a bulleted list

CHANGING TYPE SIZE

In this section you will increase the size of the type in the first line of the letter.

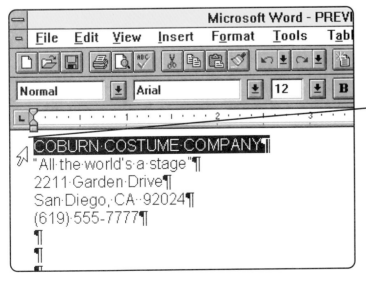

1. **Press and hold Ctrl**, then **press Home** (Ctrl + Home) to go to the top of the file if you are not already there.

2. **Click** in the **left margin** beside **Coburn Costume Company.** The line will be highlighted.

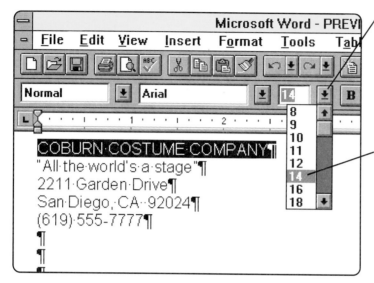

3. **Click** on ⬇ to the right of the Font Size box in the formatting toolbar. (On your screen the number 12 is in the box.) A pull-down menu will appear.

4. **Click** on **14**. The pull-down menu will disappear and the highlighted (selected) text will appear in 14-point type.

MAKING TEXT BOLD

In this section you will make the type in Coburn Costume Company boldface. You must first highlight the text you want to change. If you have been following along with the steps in this chapter, you have already highlighted Coburn Costume Company.

1. **Click** on the **Bold button** (the capital B) in the formatting toolbar. The selected text will appear in boldface type.

Notice that the Bold button appears pressed in and lighter in color. This tells you that the selected text is now bold. The Bold button works like a toggle switch. Once the text is selected, click on the Bold button to turn it on. Click on it again to turn it off.

MAKING TEXT ITALIC

In this section you will add italics to the quote in the letterhead address.

1. **Click** in the **left margin** beside **"All the world's a stage."** The line will be highlighted.

2. **Click** on the **Italics button** (the large slanted I) in the formatting toolbar. The selected text will appear in italics. Notice that the Italics button appears pressed in and lighter in color. The Italics button also works like a toggle switch.

UNDERLINING TEXT

1. **Click** on the ⬇ in the scroll bar until you can see the "We hope" sentence.

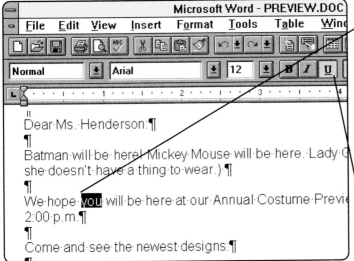

2. **Place** the **mouse pointer** to the **left** of the word **"you."** The pointer will become an I-beam. **Click** to set it in place.

3. **Press and hold** the mouse button and **drag** the pointer over the word **"you."** It will be highlighted.

4. **Click** on the **Underline button** in the formatting toolbar.

CENTERING TEXT

In this section you will center all four lines at the top of the page. You can highlight all of the lines and apply the centering command to all four at the same time. You will then center two other portions of text in the letter.

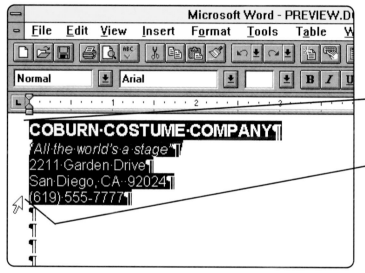

1. Press and hold Ctrl, then **press Home** (Ctrl + Home) to get back to the beginning of the file.

2. Click in the **left margin** beside **"Coburn Costume Company."** to highlight it.

3. Press and hold the **Shift key** and **click** in the **left margin** beside **"(619) 555-7777."** All the lines between clicks will be highlighted.

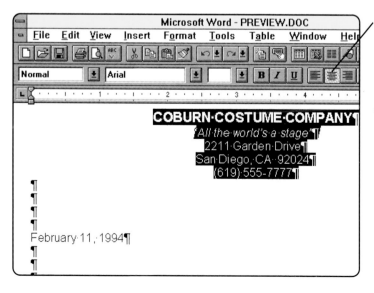

4. Click on the **Center button** in the formatting toolbar. The highlighted text will be centered across the page. Notice that the Center button appears pressed in and lighter in color. (The Center button does *not* work like a toggle switch. You have to click on another text alignment button to change the alignment.)

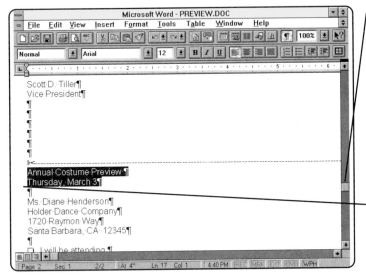

5. **Click and hold** on the scroll button and **drag** it about two-thirds of the way down the scroll bar so that it looks like the one in this example.

6. **Click** in the **left margin** beside **Annual Costume Preview** to highlight it.

7. **Press and hold** the **Shift key** and **click** in the **left margin** beside **Thursday, March 3.** Both lines will be highlighted.

8. **Click** on the **Center button** in the formatting toolbar. Both lines will be centered across the page.

9. **Press and hold** the **Ctrl key,** then **press** the **End key** (Ctrl + End). You will go to the end of the letter.

10. **Repeat steps 6 to 8** to center the last two lines of the letter.

11. **Click** on the **Save tool** in the toolbar to save your work.

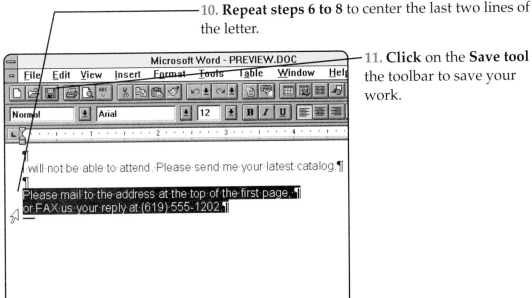

"READING" THE RIBBON

When you move the insertion point to the beginning of a paragraph, the settings in the ribbon will reflect the formatting or styles in the paragraph. In this section you will see how the ribbon reflects the formatting of "Coburn Costume Company."

1. Press and hold the **Ctrl key**, then **press** the **Home key** (Ctrl + Home) to return to the top of the letter.

Notice the settings on the ribbon:

❖ Normal is the standard style of all Word documents. You can change this style. Since most of your work will be done in this style, this is the style used in this introduction to Word.

❖ Arial and 14 points are the font and point size of this paragraph. If you select a paragraph that has two different fonts and/or two different sizes of type, Word will show the setting of the first word in the paragraph.

❖ The Bold button is pressed in and light colored. This shows that the paragraph is bold.

❖ The Center button is pressed in and light colored. This shows that the paragraph is centered across the page.

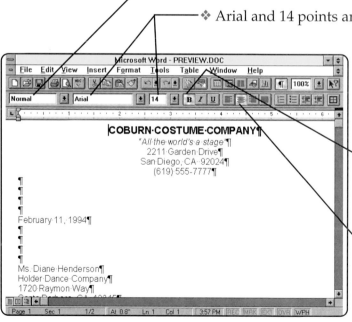

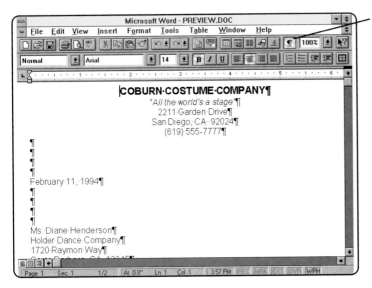

❖ When the Paragraph symbol in the standard toolbar is pressed in, the formatting marks show.

If you ever have an occasion when your type doesn't behave the way you expect it to, pay attention to these buttons. Chances will be that you clicked on a button for one paragraph and forgot to click it off for the next paragraph.

MAKING A BULLETED LIST

In this section you will make the four paragraphs that discuss the costumes that Coburn Costume Company has available into a list with bullets. It's as easy as clicking your mouse.

1. **Click** on the **scroll bar** until you can see the four paragraphs that describe the costumes.

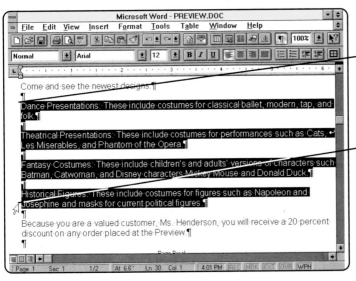

2. **Click** in the **left margin** beside **"Dance Presentations."** The line will be highlighted.

3. **Press and hold** the **Shift key** as you **click** in the **left margin** beside **"Josephine and masks..."** All the lines between the clicks will be highlighted.

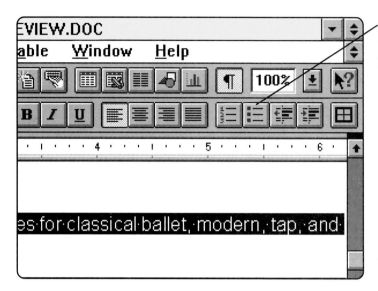

4. Click on the **Bulleted List tool** on the right of the Formatting toolbar.

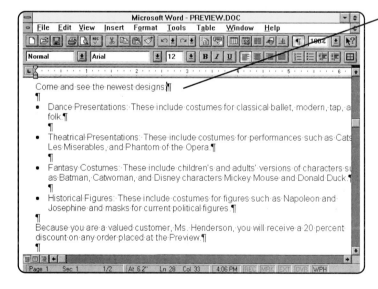

5. Click anywhere on the document to remove the highlighting so you can see the bulleted list.

Pretty terrific, don't you think?

INSERTING CHECK BOXES

You can insert a check box the same way you inserted the scissors in Chapter 1. However, you can use the bullets function as a short cut.

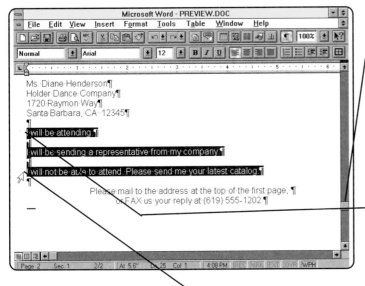

1. Click and hold on the scroll button and **drag** it three-quarters of the way down the scroll bar. You should be able to see the three reply sentences at the end of the letter.

2. Click in the **left margin** beside **"I will be attending."** to highlight the sentence.

3. Press and hold the **Shift key** and **click** in the **left margin** beside **"I will not be able to attend."** All three lines will be highlighted.

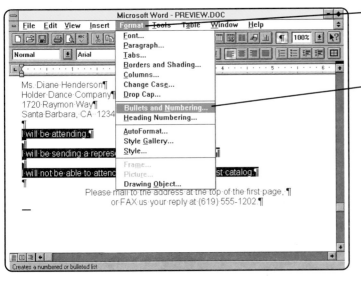

4. Click on **Format** in the menu bar. A pull-down menu will appear.

5. Click on **Bullets and Numbering**. The Bullets and Numbering dialog box will appear.

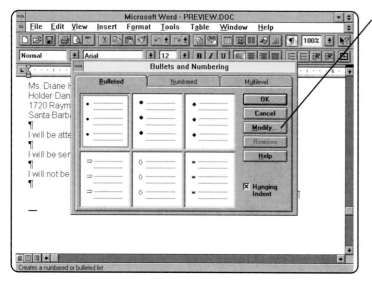

6. Click on **Modify**. The Modify Bulleted List dialog box will appear.

7. Click on the **Check Boxes** to place a selection border around it.

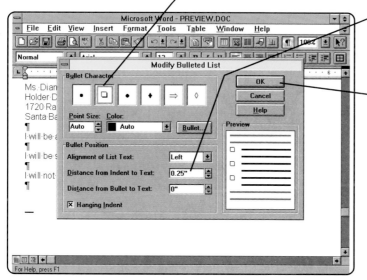

Notice that the indent from the bullet to the text is set at .25 inches.

8. Click on **OK**. The dialog box will disappear and the highlighted paragraphs will appear with check boxes.

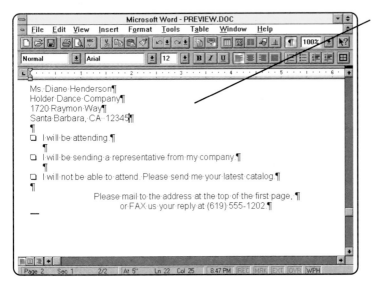

9. Click anywhere on the document to remove the highlighting from the sentences.

REMOVING BULLETS

In this example you will remove the last check box on page 2.

1. Click to the **left** of **"I will not"** in the last sentence with a check box. (Notice that you cannot click to the left of the check box.)

2. Click on **Format** in the menu bar. A pull-down menu will appear.

3. Click on **Bullets and Numbering**. The Bullets and Numbering dialog box will appear.

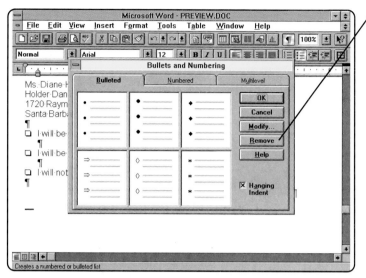

4. **Click** on **Remove**. The dialog box will close and the check box will be removed from the sentence.

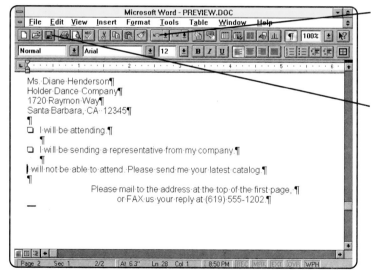

5. **Click** on the **Undo button** on the standard toolbar to put the check box back in the sentence again.

6. **Click** on the **Save button** on the standard toolbar to save your work.

Adding Pictures and Shaded Borders, and Drawing a Line

You can easily create exciting effects in Word 6. There are some wonderful clip art pictures you can use to add interest to your documents. You can put a border around text and then add shading inside the border. Word 6 also has an impressive drawing program. In this chapter you will do the following:

❖ Insert clip art into a document
❖ Draw a line with the Drawing toolbar
❖ Put a border around text
❖ Add shading inside the border

WORKING WITH CLIP ART

In this section you will select a picture (a piece of clip art) from the Clip Art directory in Word 6 and insert it into a document.

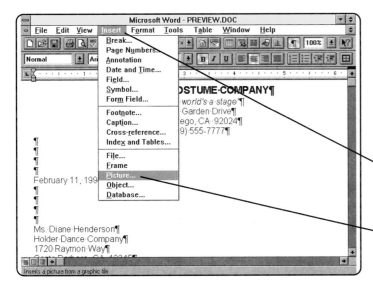

1. **Press and hold** the **Ctrl key** and **press** the **Home key** (Ctrl + Home) to go to the top of the file. In this example it's important that your cursor be at the beginning of the file.

2. **Click** on **Insert** in the menu bar. A pull-down menu will appear.

3. **Click** on **Picture**. The Insert Picture dialog box will appear.

4. Click on **1stplace.wmf**. You will see a preview of the picture on the right.

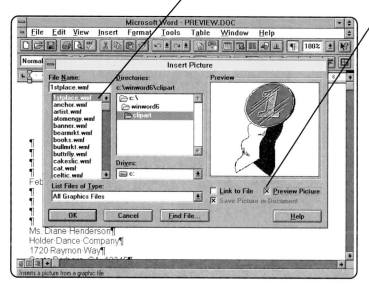

5. If you do not see the preview, **click** on **Preview Picture** to insert an X in the box. The picture will then appear in the preview area.

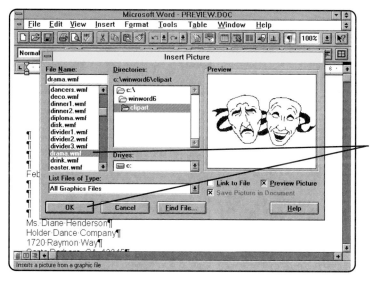

6. **Press** the ↓ on your keyboard to scroll down the list of pictures. You will see each picture in the Preview box as you highlight it in the list.

7. W**hen you have highlighted drama.wmf, click** on **OK**. The dialog box will close and the picture will appear in your letter at the cursor position.

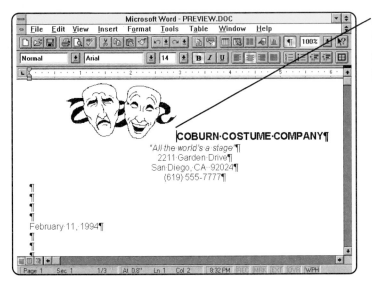

Notice that the graphic is inserted ahead of the text. In the next section you'll fix that.

INSERTING A FRAME

When you insert a graphic (piece of clip art) into a document, it is considered a separate line and displaces the text where it is placed. In this section you will put a frame around the graphic. This will cause the text to wrap (move) to the right of the graphic.

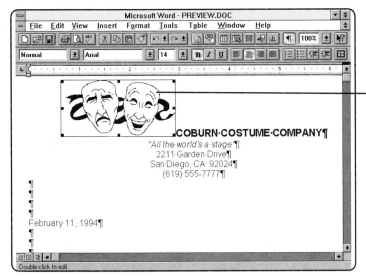

1. **Click** on the **graphic**. It will be surrounded by a selection border. A selection border has eight little squares, or handles, on its perimeter and is used to resize a graphic.

2. Click on **Insert** in the menu bar. A pull-down menu will appear.

3. Click on **Frame**. A Microsoft Word message box will appear.

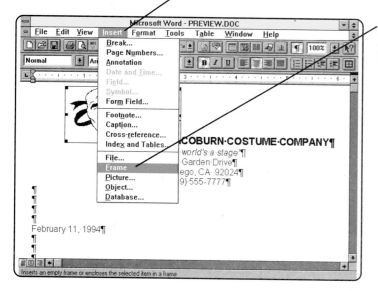

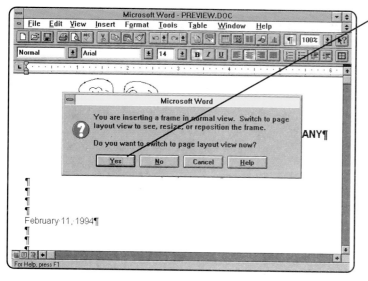

4. Click on **Yes** to switch to page layout view. This is a view that shows the placement of the graphic in relation to the text as it will be on the printed page. However, page layout view is slower for editing and scrolling.

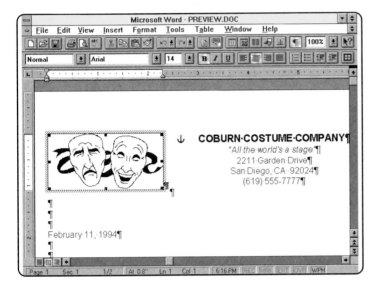

While the graphic is surrounded by the frame and selection border you can click and hold on the graphic and move it around the page. See Chapter 20, "Making a Customized Template," for more information on sizing and moving clip art.

DRAWING A LINE

In this section you will use Word's drawing program. Because drawn objects are not visible in the normal view, you should be in the page layout view. If you

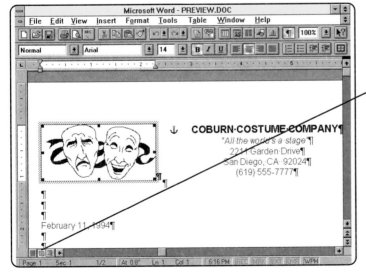

have been following along with this chapter, you are already in page layout view.

1. **Click** on the **Page Layout button** at the bottom of your screen, if you are not already in page layout view. It will look pressed in and lighter in color.

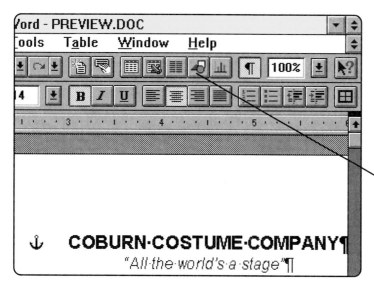

Opening the Drawing Toolbar

Word 6 has a special toolbar for the drawing program.

1. Click on the **Drawing button** on the standard toolbar. The drawing toolbar will appear at the bottom of your screen.

Selecting the Line

Now that the drawing toolbar is open, you need to tell Word what kind of line you want to draw. In this example, you will select a single line with a shadow.

1. Click on the **Line Style button** on the toolbar. A pop-up box of line styles will appear.

2. Click on **More** to see the Drawing Defaults dialog box.

Notice that the Weight shows .75 pt., which is a thin line. (In this book, the line that points to Weight is a 1 point line.)

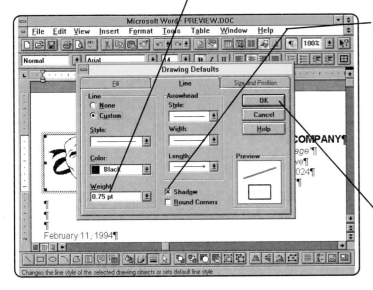

3. **Click** on **Shadow** to insert an X in the box. (This will stay selected until you change it. So, the next time you draw a line it will have a shadow unless you click on this box again to remove the X before you draw the line.)

4. **Click** on **OK** to close the dialog box.

5. **Click** on the **Line tool** on the toolbar.

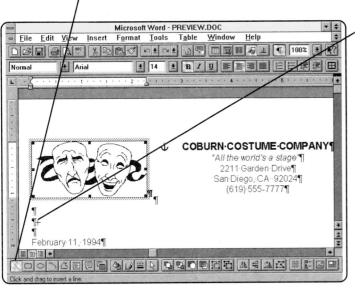

6. **Click two lines above the date** to place the cursor. The cursor will be in the shape of a plus sign (+).

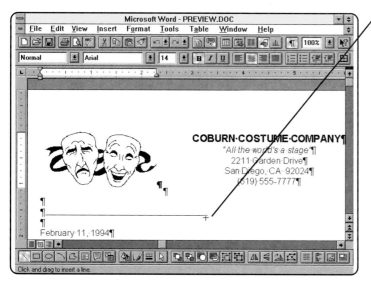

7. Press and hold the **mouse button** and **drag** the cursor across the page in a straight line. If the line gets off course and becomes jagged, simply fiddle with the placement of the mouse a little until the line straightens out again.

8. Drag the line to the **right edge of the screen**. Then **release** the **mouse button**. You will see a thin line with a second shadow line underneath it.

Removing the Drawing Toolbar

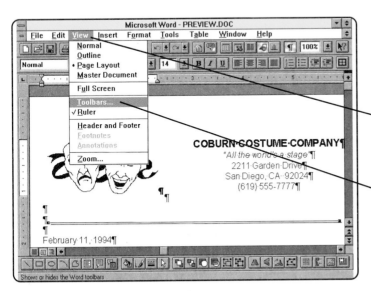

You won't need the drawing toolbar for the next section, so remove it from your screen.

1. **Click** on **View** in the menu bar. A pull-down menu will appear.

2. **Click** on **Toolbars**. The Toolbars dialog box will appear.

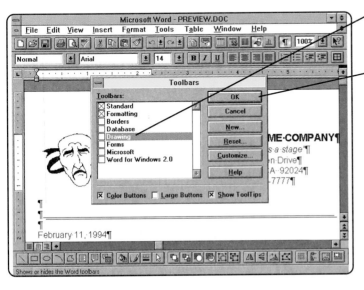

3. **Click** on **Drawing** to *remove* the X from the box.

4. **Click** on **OK**. The dialog box will close and the toolbar will be removed from your screen.

CHANGING THE ALIGN-MENT OF THE PICTURE

1. Click on the **Full-Page View button** (normal view) at the bottom of the screen. The screen will return to the normal view.

Remember, you can't see drawn objects in normal view, so you won't see the line you drew. Also, the picture appears in a different place than you see in page layout view. This is because the picture has taken on the center alignment of the text. In this example, you will change the alignment of the picture to left alignment.

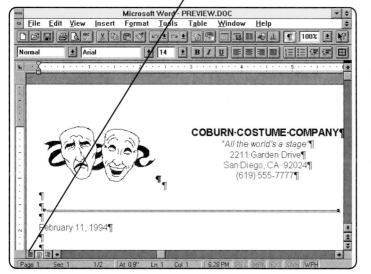

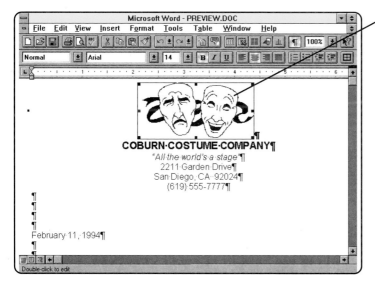

2. Click on the **picture**. It will be surrounded by a selection border.

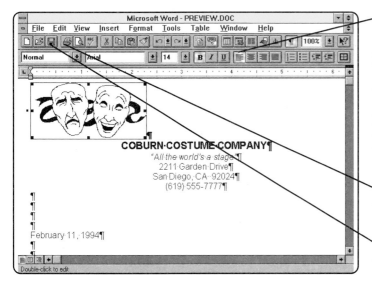

3. Click on the **Left-alignment button**. The picture will move to the left.

You cannot print when you are in Page Layout view so here's your chance to see what the letter looks like.

4. Click on the **Print button** to print the letter.

5. Click on the **Save button** to save your work.

ADDING A SHADED BORDER AROUND TEXT

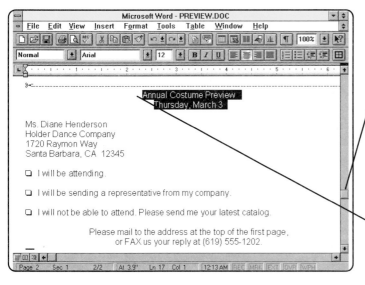

In this section, you will add a shaded border around the heading on the reply form on page 2.

1. Click and hold on the scroll button and **drag** it two-thirds of the way down the scroll bar. You should be able to see the scissors.

2. Click to the **left** of **Annual Costume Preview** to highlight the line.

3. Press and hold the **Shift key** and **click** to the left of **Thursday, March 3**. Both lines will be highlighted.

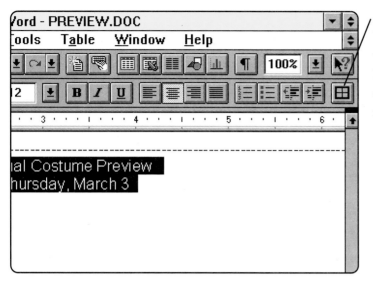

4. Click on the **Border button** on the far right of the formatting toolbar. The borders toolbar will appear on your screen above the ruler.

5. Click on the **Outside Border button**. A border that is ¾ pt. wide will appear around the highlighted text. (See the ¾ pt. indicator on the left of the toolbar.)

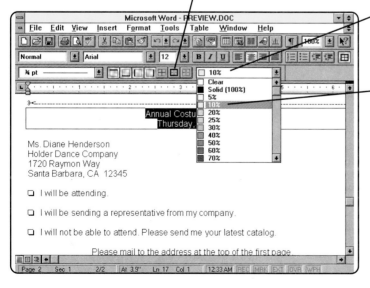

6. Click on the **Shading button** on the toolbar. A pull-down list will appear.

7. Click on **10%**. The pull-down menu will disappear and the border will appear with a light 10% shading.

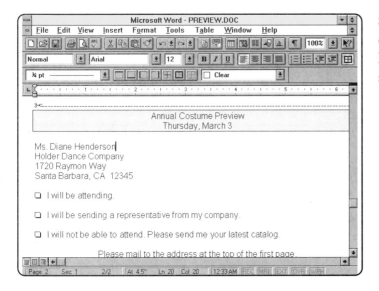

8. Click anywhere on the document to remove the highlighting and see the shaded border.

REMOVING A SHADED BORDER

To remove a shaded border, you must first highlight the text inside the border.

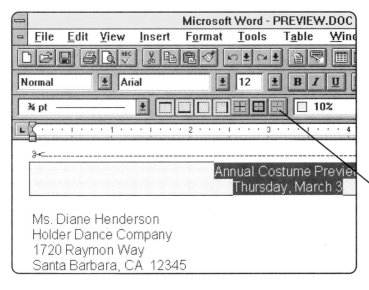

1. Click to the left of **Annual Costume Preview** to highlight the line.

2. Press and hold the **Shift key** and **click** to the left of the date line to highlight both lines.

3. Click on the **No Border button** on the toolbar to remove the border.

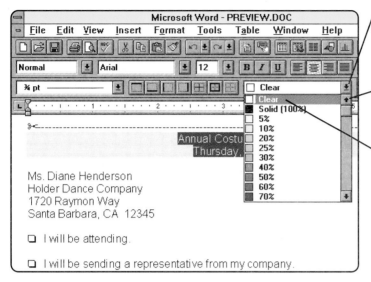

4. Click on the ⬇ to the right of the Shading box. A pull-down list will appear.

5. Click on the ⬆ to scroll up to Clear.

6. Click on **Clear**. The shading will be removed.

UNDOING TWO PREVIOUS STEPS

You can reverse the last two steps you took to remove the border and the shading.

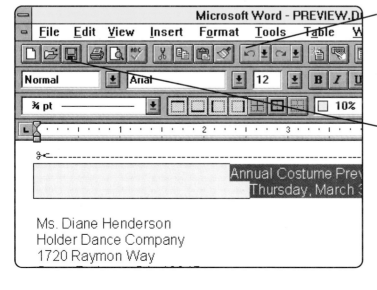

1. Click two times on the Undo button. The first click will replace the shading and the second click will replace the outside border.

2. Click on the **Save button** to save your work.

Setting and Applying Tabs

Word for Windows 6 has tabs pre-set at every half inch. To insert a tab, simply press the Tab key. You can also set your own tabs. When you set a tab, the preset tabs between the new tab and the left margin disappear. In this chapter you will set and apply the following kinds of tabs:

❖ The standard *left-aligned tab* that lines words up on the first letter: Josh

    Jessica

❖ A *leader* (line) that ends at a *right-aligned tab*:   Josh _____

    Jessica ____

❖ A *right-aligned tab* that aligns words on the last letter: Josh

    Jessica

❖ A *center-aligned tab* that centers words: Josh

    Jessica

❖ A *decimal tab* that aligns numbers on the decimal point: 9.50

    99.50

GETTING READY TO SET TABS

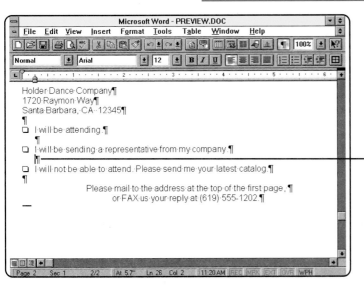

1. Click on the scroll bar to go to the end of the PREVIEW.DOC letter, if you are not already there. You should be able to see the three check boxes at the end of the letter.

2 Click on the **blank line** above the last check box.

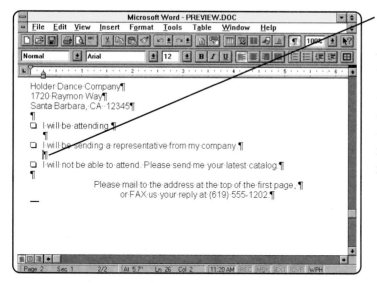

Notice that the paragraph symbol is indented to align with the typed sentence. This is because the three sentences have been formatted as a bulleted list and the bulleted list feature is set to have a .25-inch indent.

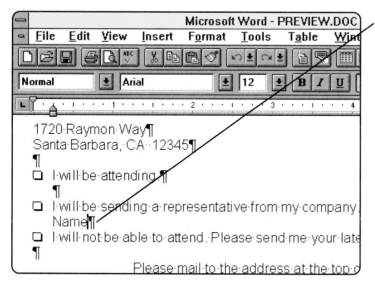

3. **Type Name**. Notice the paragraph mark moves as you type.

INSERTING A LEADER WITH A RIGHT-ALIGNED TAB

A common example of a leader is the dotted line in a table of contents that connects a chapter and its page number, as shown here:

Chapter 2...34

Another common example of a leader is the fill-in-the-blank solid line seen on forms, for example:

Name_____

To create these kinds of leaders, use the Right-Aligned Tab button.

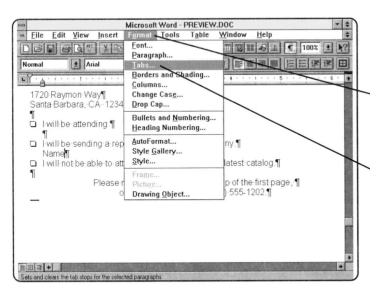

In this section you will insert a solid line after "Name."

1. **Click** on **Format** in the menu bar. A pull-down menu will appear.

2 **Click** on **Tabs**. The Tabs dialog box will appear.

3. **Type 4** to set a tab at 4 inches.

4 **Click** on **Right** to put a dot in the circle.

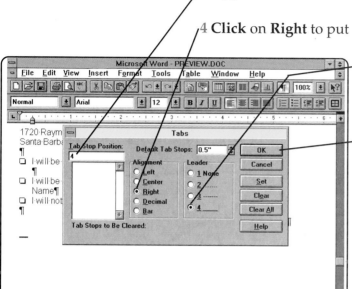

5. **Click** on **Option 4** (the solid line option) to insert a dot in the circle.

6. **Click** on **OK**. The dialog box will close and a right-aligned tab will appear in the ruler at 4 inches.

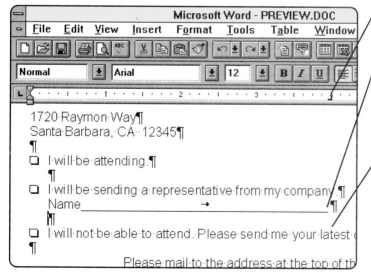

Notice the right-aligned tab mark at 4 inches.

7. **Press** the **Tab key**. The paragraph mark will move to the 4-inch mark and a line will appear in the text.

8. **Press** the **Enter key** to move the cursor to the next line.

SOME NOTES ABOUT TABS

Note 1: When you set a tab in an already-typed document, the tab applies *only* to the paragraph in which you set it. In this example, you added a second line to the paragraph that contains the tab by pressing the Enter key at the end of the line. Therefore, the tab that you set at 4 inches still applies to this new line. It does not, however, apply to any other paragraph. If you want a tab to apply to more that one paragraph, highlight all appropriate paragraphs before you set the tab.

Note 2: When you set a tab, it erases all preset tabs between it and the left margin. In the previous example, the tab you set at 4 inches erased the tabs that are preset every half-inch. In this next example, you will set a left-aligned tab .5 inches from the left margin.

SETTING A LEFT-ALIGNED TAB

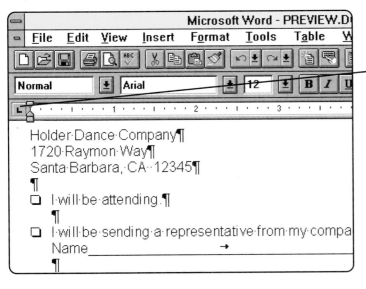

You can use a mouse to set a tab directly in the ruler.

1. **Confirm** that the left-aligned tab mark appears on the tab button on the ruler.

2. **Place** the mouse pointer in the ruler (it will become an arrow) so that the arrow points at, but does not touch, the **.5-inch mark** on the ruler.

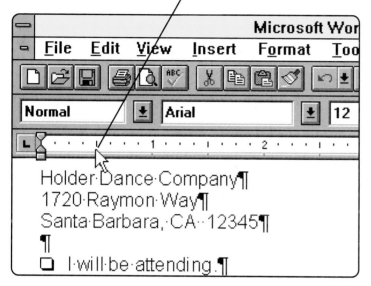

3 **Click** the mouse button. A left-aligned tab mark will appear just below the .5-inch mark on the ruler line. If the tab mark does not appear, you probably placed the arrow too close to the .5-inch mark. Try again.

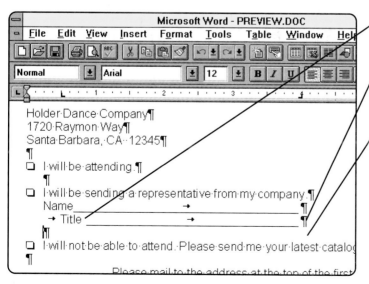

4. **Press** the **Tab key** and **type Title**.

5. **Press** the **Tab key** to insert a solid line.

6. **Press Enter** to move the cursor to the next line.

CLEARING A TAB

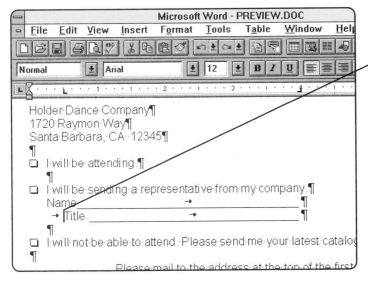

You'll love how easy it is to clear a tab.

1. Click to the **left of "Title"** to place the cursor.

2 Press the **Backspace key**. "Title" will backspace one tab position and be aligned under "Name." Notice that the leader line extends to fill the space.

Now you will clear the tab you set at .5 inch.

3. Place the arrow **on top of the left-aligned tab mark** and **press and hold** the mouse button. You will see a dotted line in the document at the tab position.

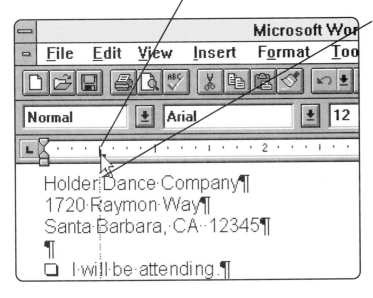

4. Continue to **press and hold** the mouse button and **drag** the tab mark down into the document.

5. Release the mouse button. The tab will be removed from the ruler. Isn't this a really cool feature?!

6 Press and hold the **Ctrl key** then **type** the letter **s** (Ctrl + s). This is another way to save your work.

OPENING A NEW DOCUMENT

In the remaining sections of the chapter, you'll learn how to set a right-aligned tab and a center-aligned tab with the mouse, and set a decimal tab with the mouse and from the menu bar. Since the tabs will not be used in PREVIEW.DOC, you will open a new document. You don't need to close PREVIEW.DOC in order to open a new document though. Word allows multiple documents to be open at the same time.

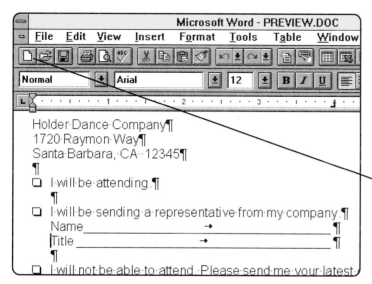

1. Click on the **New Document button** on the toolbar. A new document will appear on your screen on top of PREVIEW.DOC.

CHANGING LINE SPACING

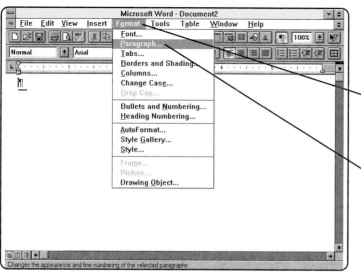

In this section you will change the line spacing from single to double.

1. Click on **Format** on the menu bar. A pull-down menu will appear.

2. Click on **Paragraph**. The Paragraph dialog box will appear.

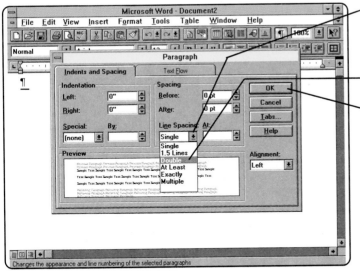

3 **Click** on the ⬇ to the right of Single. A drop-down list will appear.

4. **Click** on **Double**.

5. **Click** on **OK**. The dialog box will close. You are now set to type with double spacing. When you press Enter, the cursor will automatically go down two lines.

SETTING A RIGHT-ALIGNED TAB

1. **Click two times** on the **Tab button** on the ruler to change the setting from the left-aligned tab symbol to the right-aligned tab symbol you see in this example.

2. **Place** the mouse pointer in the lower-half of the ruler **at the .5-inch mark**. It will become an arrow.

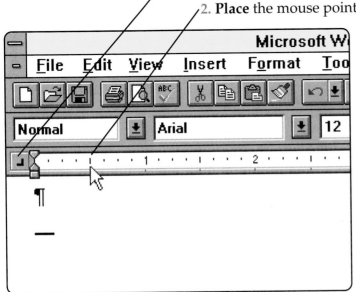

3. **Click** to insert a right-aligned tab at this position. (If the tab mark does not appear, you probably placed the arrow too close to the ruler line. Move the arrow slightly and try again.)

You will use this tab setting later in the chapter in the section "Applying Tabs."

SETTING A CENTER-ALIGNED TAB

In this section you will use the mouse to set a center-aligned tab at the 2-inch mark.

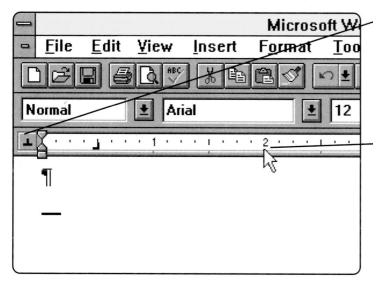

1. **Click three times** on the **Tab button** in the ruler to change the setting from the right-aligned symbol to the center-aligned symbol you see in this example.

2. **Place** the mouse pointer in the lower-half of the ruler at the **2-inch mark**. Do not let the arrow touch the 2-inch mark.

3. **Click** to set the center-aligned tab in place.

You will use this tab setting later in the chapter in the section "Applying Tabs."

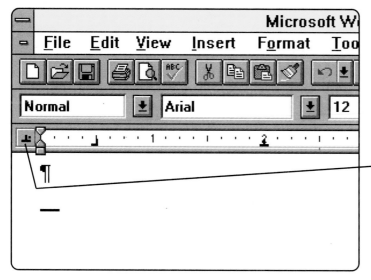

SETTING A DECIMAL TAB

In this section you will use the mouse to set a decimal tab at 3.5 inches.

1. **Click two times** on the **Tab button** to change the setting from the center-aligned symbol to the decimal symbol you see in this example.

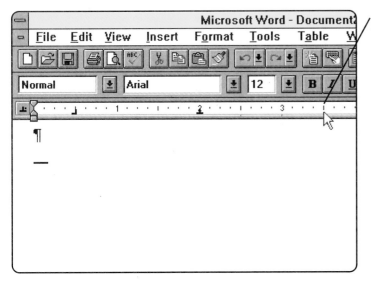

2. Place the mouse pointer in the lower-half of the ruler at the **3.5-inch mark**. Do not let the arrow touch the vertical mark.

3 Click to set the decimal tab in place.

You will use this tab setting later in the chapter in the section "Applying Tabs."

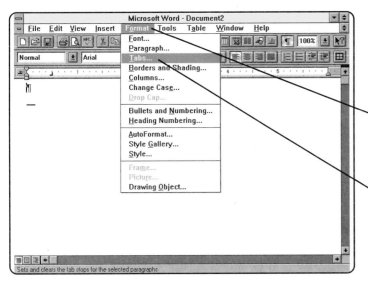

In the next part of this section you will use the Tab Set dialog box to set a second decimal tab.

1. Click on **Format** in the menu bar. A pull-down menu will appear.

2. Click on **Tabs**. The Tabs dialog box will appear.

Notice that the tabs you set with the mouse are listed in the Tab Stop Position list box.

3. **Type 5.** It will replace the highlighted 0.5" in the Tab Stop Position box.

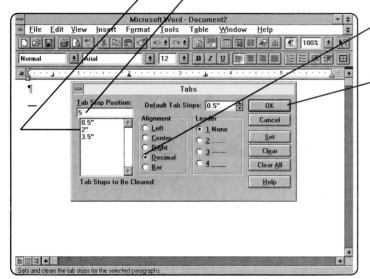

4. **Click** on **Decimal** to place a dot in the circle.

5. **Click** on **OK** to set a tab and close the dialog box.

APPLYING TABS

In this section you will apply the tabs you set in the previous sections. Because you set the tabs at the beginning of a blank document, they will apply from this point on until you reset them. As you type, notice how each text entry aligns on the tab stop in the ruler.

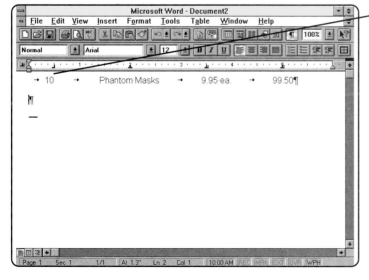

1. **Press Tab** and **type 10.**

2. **Press Tab** and **type Phantom Masks.** Notice that the text moves backwards as you type.

3. **Press Tab** and **type 9.95 ea.**

4 **Press Tab** and **type 99.50.**

5. **Press Enter.** The cursor will move down two lines.

6. **Press Tab** and **type 5**. Notice the "5" is right-aligned under "10."

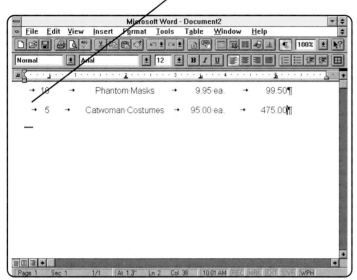

7. **Press Tab** and **type Catwoman costumes**. Notice that it is centered under the entry above it.

8. **Press Tab** and **type 95.00 ea.** Notice that the decimal points are lined up.

9. **Press Tab** and **type 475.00**. Again, notice that the decimal points are lined up.

SWITCHING BETWEEN OPEN DOCUMENTS

In this section you will switch back and forth between the unnamed file on your screen and PREVIEW.

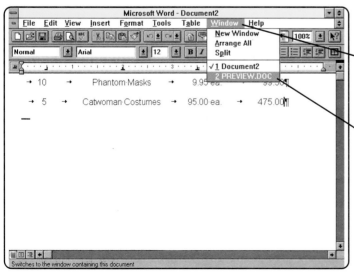
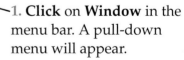
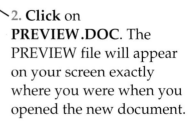

1. **Click** on **Window** in the menu bar. A pull-down menu will appear.

2. **Click** on **PREVIEW.DOC**. The PREVIEW file will appear on your screen exactly where you were when you opened the new document.

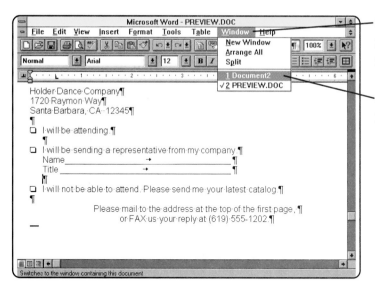

3. **Click** on **Window** in the menu bar. A pull-down menu will appear.

4. **Click** on **Document2** to return to the tab document.

CLOSING WITHOUT SAVING

Because this exercise was meant only as practice in setting different types of tabs and will not be used later in the book, you don't need to save the document.

1. **Click** on **File** in the menu bar. A pull-down menu will appear.

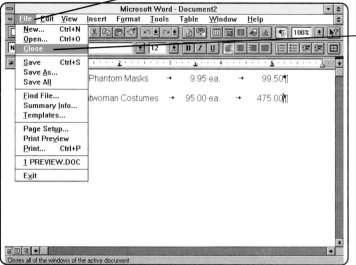

2. **Click** on **Close**. Because you have not saved this document, you will see a Microsoft Word dialog box asking if you want to save the document.

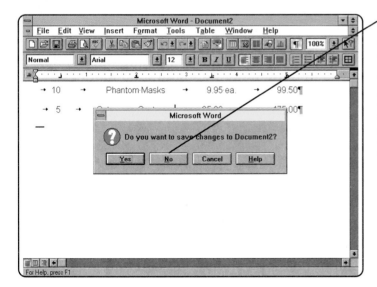

3. **Click** on **No**. The document will close without being saved. You will see PREVIEW.DOC on your screen. It will be exactly as you left it when you opened the new document.

Adding a Section Divider, Header, and Page Number

In Word for Windows 6 you can divide a document into sections and format each section separately, allowing you to make elements like margins, headers, and footers different in each section. A *header* is information that is printed at the top of the page. For example, in this book the page number and book title is a header on every left page and the chapter title and page number is a header on every right page. In this chapter you will do the following:

❖ Make page 2 of the sample PREVIEW.DOC file into a separate section and change the top margin

❖ Insert a header on page 2 of the sample document

❖ Insert a page number on page 2

SEPARATING A DOCUMENT INTO TWO SECTIONS

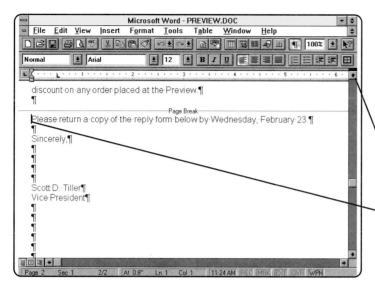

In this section, you will change the top margin on page 2. To do this you will make page 2 a separate section.

1. **Click** on ⬆ to scroll up so that you can see the end of page 1.

2. **Click** to the **left** of **"Please return"** at the top of page 2.

3. **Click** on **File** in the menu bar. A pull-down menu will appear.

4. **Click** on **Page Setup**. The Page Setup dialog box will appear.

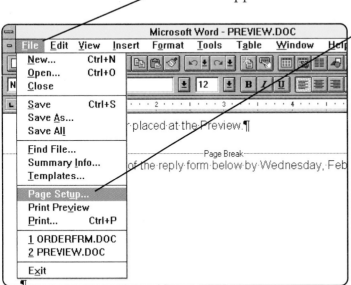

5. **Click** on **Margins** if it is not already the front "card" in the dialog box.

6. **Click twice** on the ▲ to the **right** of the **Top Margin box** to change it to 1".

7. **Click** on the ▼ to the right of the Apply To box. A pull-down list will appear.

8. **Click** on **This Point Forward** to change the margin for page 2 and create page 2 as a section.

9. **Click** on **OK** to confirm the changes you just made and close the dialog box.

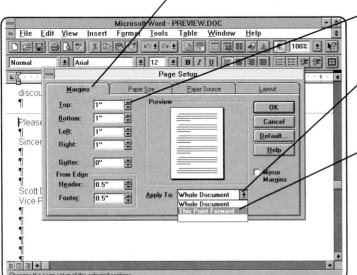

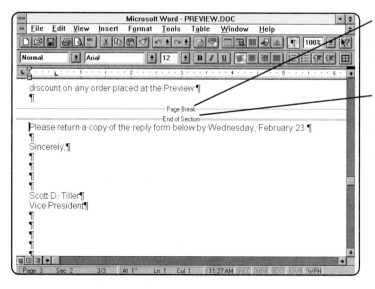

Notice that the Page Break is still there. You will delete it in the next section.

Notice the double line indicating the end of Section 1 (and the start of the new section).

Deleting the Page Break

1. **Place** the mouse pointer in the left margin **on top of the page break line**. The pointer will change to an arrow.

2. **Click** on the **page break line**. You will see a small highlight bar.

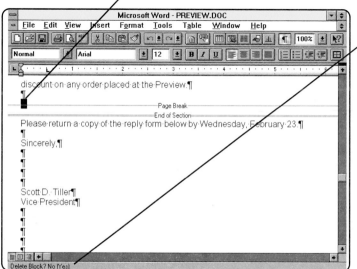

3. **Press** the **Delete key**. A question Delete Block? No (Yes) will appear in the status line.

4. **Type** the letter **y**. The page break line will disappear. The double line indicating the new section is still there. (Instead of steps 3 and 4 you could press Backspace.)

CREATING A HEADER

When you create a header in Word, it will appear at the top of every page of the document unless you tell it otherwise. Although there are several ways to do this, the following steps will be appropriate for most situations.

1. **Click** at the **bottom of page 1** to place the cursor.

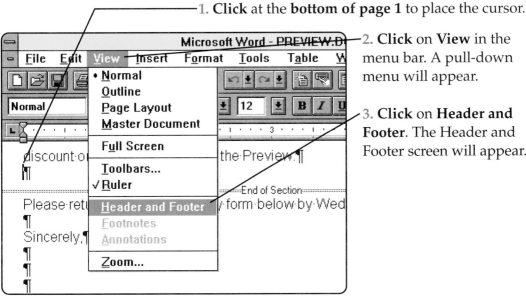

2. **Click** on **View** in the menu bar. A pull-down menu will appear.

3. **Click** on **Header and Footer**. The Header and Footer screen will appear.

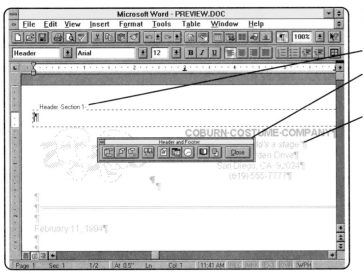

Notice the following:

❖ The Header-Section 1 box

❖ The Header and Footer toolbar

❖ The greyed-out document in the background

4. **Type Ms. Diane Henderson** and **press Enter**. The header box will expand

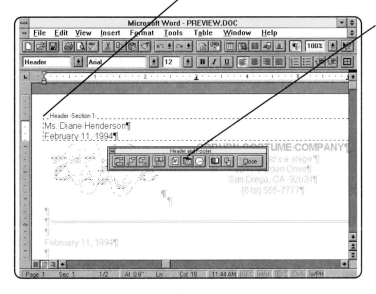

5. **Click** on the **Date button** on the toolbar. Today's date will be inserted into the Header box. (Your date may appear in a different format, e.g. 2/11/94.)

PRINTING THE HEADER ON PAGE TWO ONLY

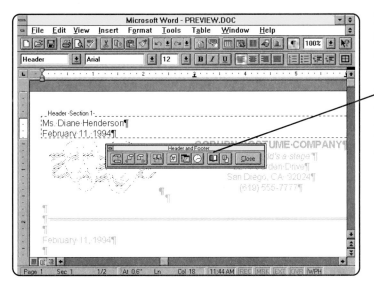

Now you have to go to Page Setup and tell Word to print the header only on page 2.

1. **Click** on the **Page Setup button** on the toolbar. The Page Setup dialog box will appear.

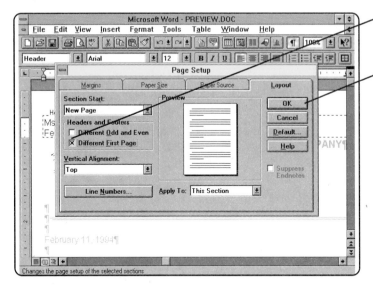

2. Click on **Different First Page** to put an X in the box.

3. Click on **OK**. The Page Setup dialog box will close and you will be returned to the header on the document.

Notice the box labeled "First Page Header-Section 1" is now empty. You can see a greyed-out page 1 in the background.

4. Click on the **Show Next button** on the Header and Footer toolbar to move to page 2.

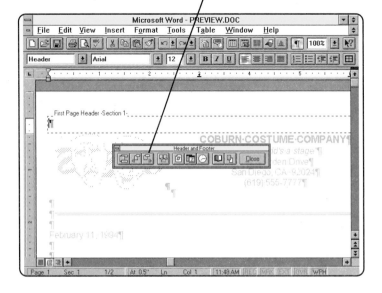

Notice the header is now labeled "Header-Section 2" and the text you typed is in the box. You can see a greyed-out page 2 in the background.

CHANGING THE DISTANCE BETWEEN THE HEADER AND THE DOCUMENT TEXT

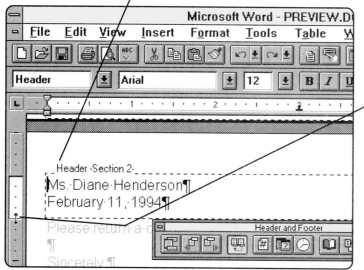

You can use your mouse to increase the distance between the header and the document text.

1. **Place** the mouse pointer on the **bottom margin boundary** on the vertical ruler. It will change to a double-headed arrow.

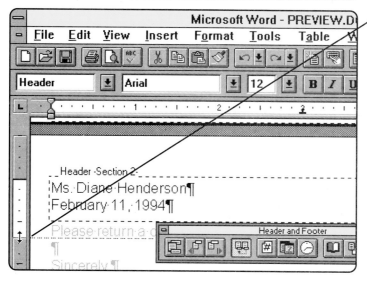

2. **Press and hold** the mouse button and **drag** the boundary down to **below** the greyed-out **"Please return"** line. Release the mouse button.

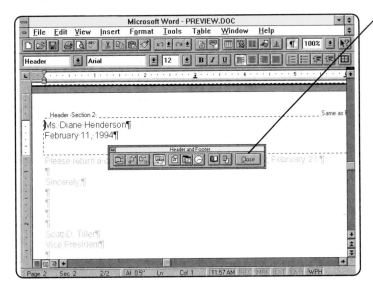

4. Click on **Close** in the Header and Footer toolbar.

Although the header will print, you will not see it in the normal view. You will change the view later in the chapter so you can see it.

ADDING A PAGE NUMBER

You can add page numbers from any point in the document, but to follow this example you should be on page 1.

1. Click anywhere on **page 1** if your cursor is not already there.

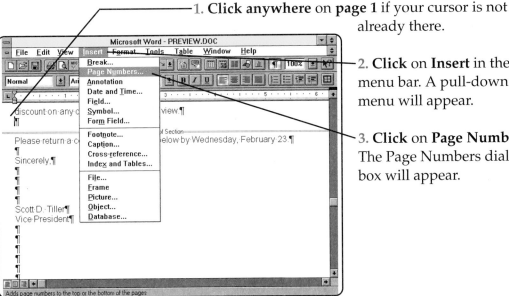

2. Click on **Insert** in the menu bar. A pull-down menu will appear.

3. Click on **Page Numbers**. The Page Numbers dialog box will appear.

4. **Confirm** that **Bottom of Page (Footer)** is in the Position box.

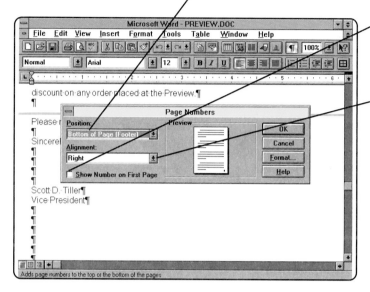

5. **Confirm** that Show Number on First Page **does** _not_ have an ✕ in the box.

6. **Click** on the ⬇ to the **right** of the **Alignment box**. A pull-down menu will appear.

7. **Click** on **Center**. The pull-down list will disappear and Center will now be in the Alignment box.

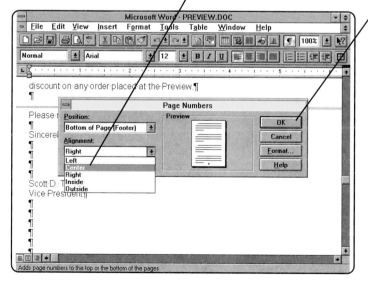

8. **Click** on **OK**. The Page Number dialog box will close and you will be returned to your normal view screen. You cannot see the page number in the normal view.

VIEWING THE HEADER
AND PAGE NUMBER

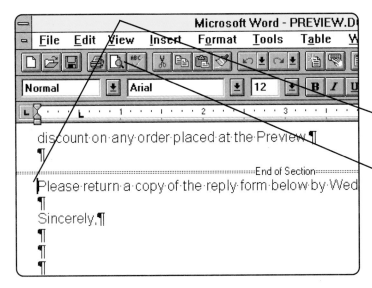

Print Preview is one of the views in which you can see the header and page number.

1. **Click** next to **"Please return"** on page 2.

2. **Click** on the **Print Preview button** on the Standard Toolbar.

Notice the header at the top of page 2 and the page number at the bottom of page 2.

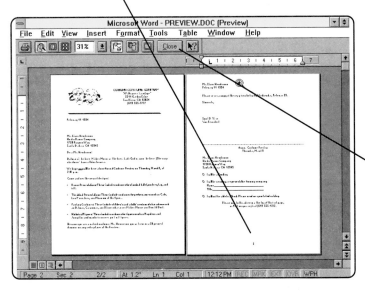

If you want to zoom in to see the header, position the magnifying glass over the header and press your left mouse button. Then press your left mouse button again to zoom out.

3. **Click** on **Close** to return to the Normal view.

4. **Press and hold** the **Ctrl key** on your keyboard and **type** the letter **s** (Ctrl + s). This is another way to save.

Using Different Views

In Word for Windows 6 you can view your document in several different ways. If you have been following the examples in this book you have already used Print Preview and Page Layout to view your document. There are other views that give different perspectives of your document. In this chapter you will do the following:

❖ View PREVIEW.DOC in Page Layout
❖ View PREVIEW.DOC in Page Width using the Zoom Control button
❖ View PREVIEW.DOC at 50%

USING THE VIEW BUTTONS

There are three different buttons in the status line that provide you three different views of your document.

❶ Clicking on this button puts the screen in the Normal View, which is the one you have used throughout this book. It is the view you see when you open Word 6.

❷ Clicking on this button puts the screen in the Page Layout View that you used in Chapter 8 to create the letterhead design for PREVIEW.DOC. You can see graphics, headers, footers, and page numbers in this view.

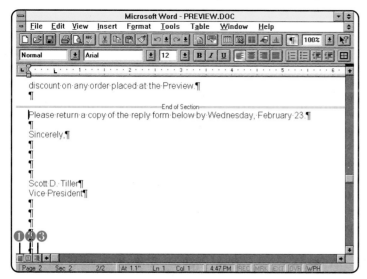

❸ Clicking on this button puts the screen in the Outline View. In this view you can collapse a document to see only the main headings or expand it to see the entire document. This view is useful for reorganizing long documents.

Using Page Layout

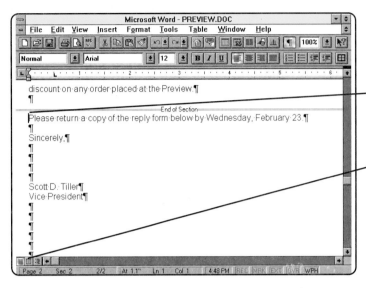

1. Click on the ↑ or ↓ in the scroll bar until you can see the top of page 2.

2. Click at the top of page 2 if your cursor is not already there.

3. Click on the **Page Layout button** just above the status bar. Your screen display will switch to Page Layout view.

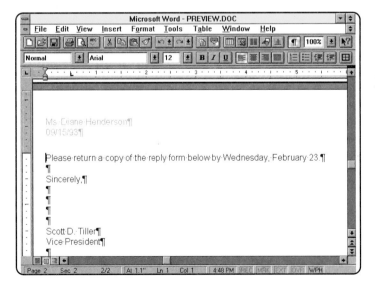

In Page Layout view you can see a document with headers and page numbers just as it will look when printed. You can edit the text and change formatting in this view.

USING THE ZOOM COMMAND

The Zoom Command controls how large or small a document appears on the screen. You can make a display larger so it is easier to read or see details, or reduce the display to view an entire page or two. The Zoom command can be used in all of the Word 6 views.

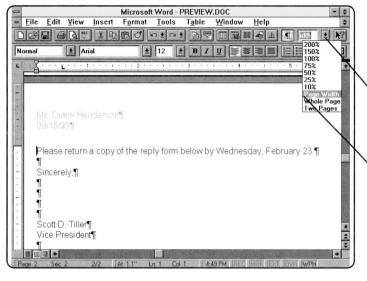

Using Page Width Zoom

1. **Click** on the ⬇ next to the Zoom Control. A drop-down list will appear.

2. **Click** on **Page Width**. The drop-down list will disappear and your document will now be shown in page width size.

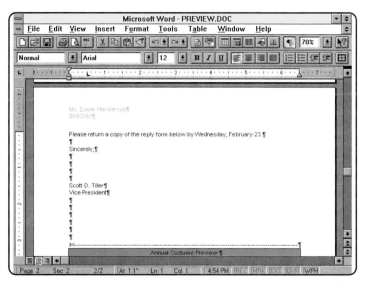

This view enables you to see the entire width of your document. Long sentences will show on the screen and will not scroll out of sight on the right side of the screen. You can work as you always do when in this view.

Using 50% Zoom

1. **Click** on the ▼ next to the Zoom Control. A drop-down list will appear.

2. **Click** on **50%**. The drop-down list will disappear and your document will appear in a 50% view.

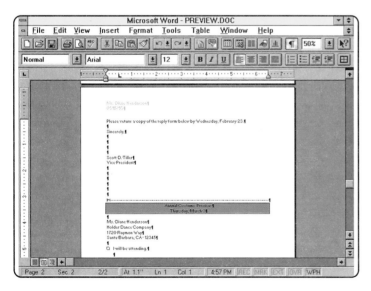

This zoom shows your document in a much reduced size and gives you a birds-eye view of your document.

Using 100% Zoom and Returning to Normal View

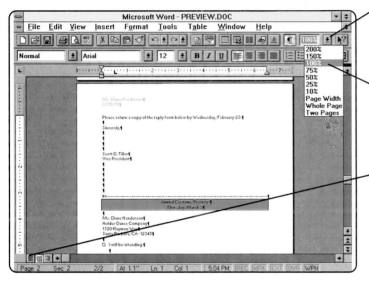

1. Click on the ⬇ next to the Zoom Control. A drop-down list will appear.

2. Click on **100%**. The drop-down list will disappear and you will be returned to a 100% view.

3. Click on the **Normal View button** above the status line. The normal view screen with which you started this chapter will reappear.

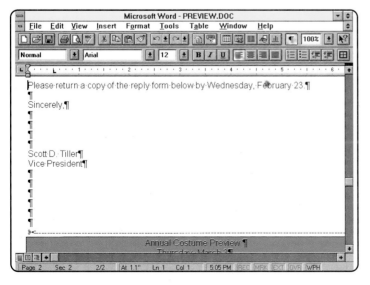

Instead of selecting a Zoom amount from the drop-down list next to the Zoom Control box, you can also Zoom to a specific percent. You simply click twice on the Zoom Control box and then type in the number of the percent you wish to zoom in or out.

Try experimenting with this and in using different views.

Program Manager

Part III   Mailing Lists, Form Letters, and Envelopes

Printing Envelopes

Word 6 makes it as easy to print an envelope as clicking your mouse. However, to customize an envelope, you must first attach it to a document before you can modify it to suit your taste. In this chapter you will do the following:

❖ Set up and print an envelope with a different font, with a bar code, and with the proper feed position for your printer

❖ Customize the return address and print the letter and the envelope at the same time

PREPARING AN ENVELOPE TO PRINT

Word 6 automatically places the user information that you entered when you installed Word into the first two lines of the initial envelope return address. The first time you use the envelope program, the two lines will appear unless you modify the user information file. In this section you will open the User Info dialog file and type a permanent address in it.

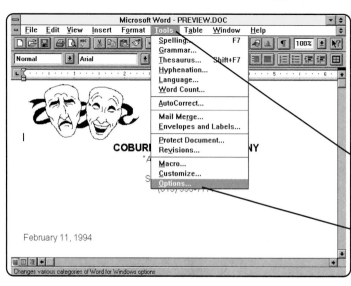

1. Open the **PREVIEW.DOC** file if it is not already on your screen.

2. Click on **Tools** in the menu bar. A pull-down menu will appear.

3. Click on **Options**. The Options dialog box will appear.

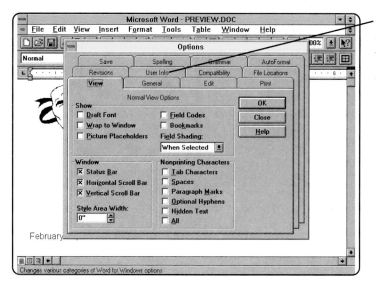

4. **Click** on the **User Info tab**. The User Info dialog box will move to the front of the Options dialog box.

Notice that the name and company you typed when you installed Word 6 automatically appears in the mailing address dialog box.

5. **Click** on the **Mailing Address box** to set the cursor in the box.

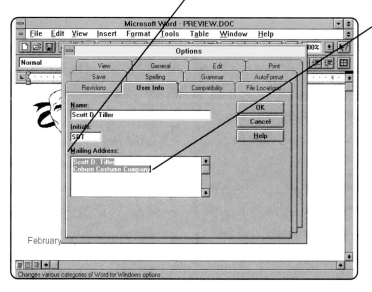

6. **Press and hold** the mouse button as you **drag** the cursor to highlight the two lines of text.

7. **Type** the following return address:

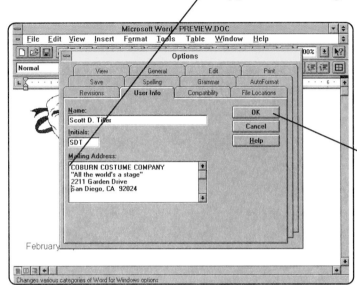

COBURN COSTUME COMPANY

"All the world's a stage"

2211 Garden Drive

San Diego, CA 92024

8. **Click** on **OK**. The PREVIEW.DOC document screen will appear.

Opening the Envelope Dialog Box

1. **Click** on **Tools** in the menu bar. A pull-down menu will appear.

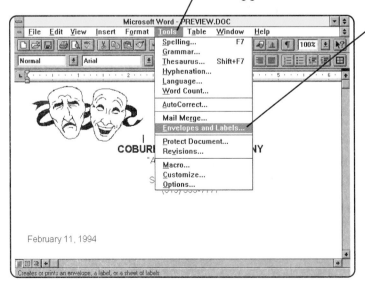

2. **Click** on **Envelopes and Labels.** The Envelopes and Labels dialog box will appear.

Notice that Word puts the mailing address in the Delivery Address text box.

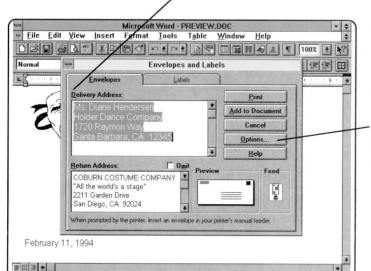

Changing the Return Address Font

1. Click on **Options**. The Envelope Options dialog box will appear.

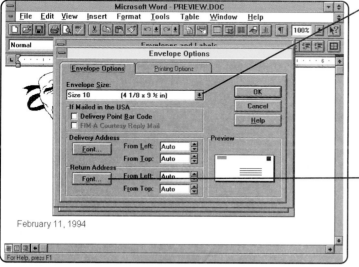

Notice that Word automatically selects the standard size business envelope for you. If you want to select another envelope size, click on ⬇ on the right of the Envelope Size box.

2. Click on the **Font button** in the Return Address dialog box. The Envelope Return Address dialog box will appear.

3. **Click** on the Font tab if it is not already in front.

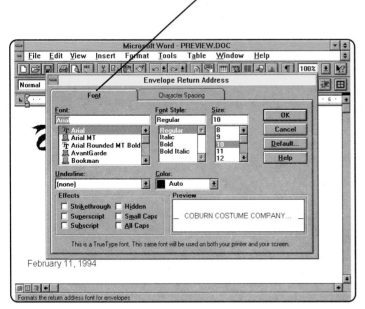

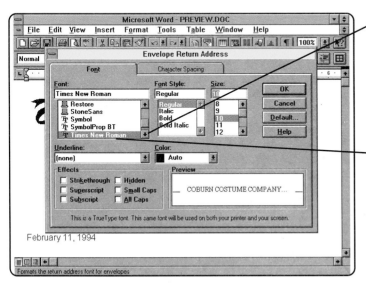

4. **Click** on ↓ on the scroll bar to scroll down the list of available fonts. Your list of fonts may be different from the one shown here.

5. **Click** on **Times New Roman**. The drop-down list box will disappear and "Times New Roman" will appear in the Font box.

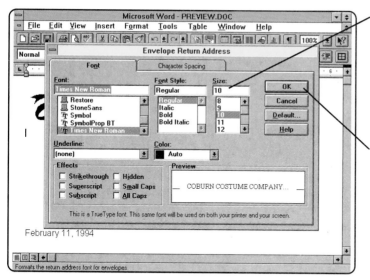

Notice that you can change the point size of the font, which you will do later in this chapter in the section entitled "Customizing the Return Address."

6. Click on **OK**. The Envelope Options dialog box will return.

Adding the Bar Code

You can add a bar code to the envelope if you want to. It is a machine-readable representation of the U.S. Zip Code and the delivery point address. Using the bar code supposedly speeds up mail delivery processing. You be the judge.

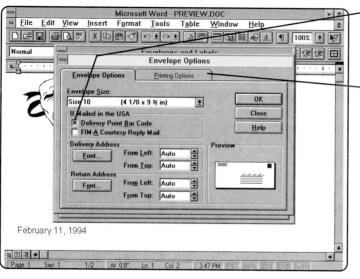

1. Click on the **Delivery Point Bar Code** to place an X in the box.

2. Click on the **Printing Options tab**. The Printing Options dialog box will appear.

Selecting the Envelope Feed Position

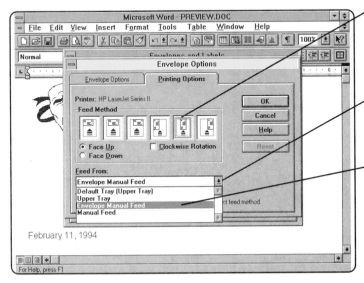

Notice that the Feed Method is automatically selected based on the current printer.

1. **Click** on ⬇ to the right of the Feed Form. A drop-down list box will appear.

2. **Click** on **Envelope Manual Feed** (or one of the other selections). The drop-down list will disappear and Envelope Manual Feed will appear in the Feed Form box.

3. **Click** on **OK**. The Envelopes and Labels dialog box will reappear.

Omitting and Restoring the Standard (Default) Return Address

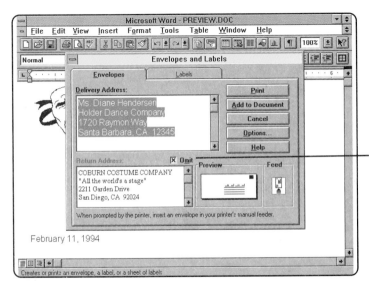

1. **Click** on **Omit** to place an X in the box if you want to omit the return address.

2. **Click** on **Omit** again to remove the X and restore the address.

PRINTING WITH A RETURN ADDRESS

Printing with a LaserJet Series II or III Printer

1. Place an **envelope tray** into your printer. If you do not have an envelope tray, place a single envelope in the **manual feed slot** on your printer's paper tray. Since each brand of printer operates slightly differently, consult your printer manual for the exact placement of the envelope as you feed it into the printer.

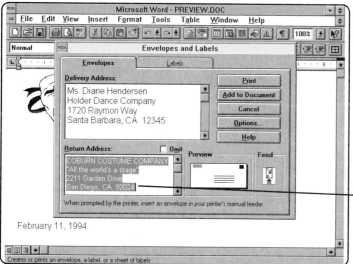

Notice that the Return Address appears in the Return Address text box. This is the address typed in the User Info text box in the first section of this chapter entitled "Preparing an Envelope to Print."

Notice that the address on your letter appears in the Delivery Address box. Word automatically searches for the address in the letter and enters it here.

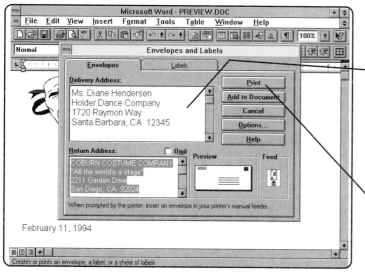

2. Click on **Print**. The Printing message box will appear.

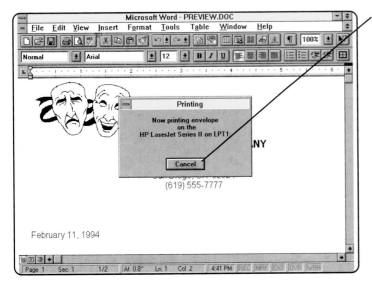

If you change your mind, **click** on **Cancel**. When the Printing message box disappears, the envelopes will begin printing. Slick!

Notice that the name of your laser printer appears in this box.

Printing with a Dot-Matrix Printer

Since each brand of printer operates slightly differently, consult your manual for the exact placement of the envelope as you feed it into the printer.

1. Remove the **tractor feed paper** from your printer and **insert** an **envelope**. Word 6 tells most dot-matrix printers to feed the envelope through half an inch before beginning to print. If you want the return address to be printed further down on the envelope, adjust the envelope's position manually before printing. Your printer may let you feed an envelope without removing the tractor feed paper.

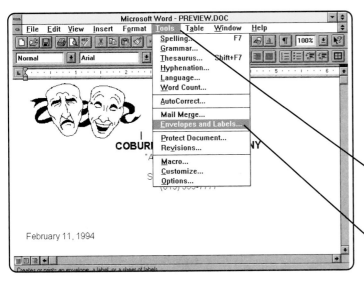

2. Click on the **Tools** in the menu bar. a pull-down menu will appear.

3. Click on Envelopes and Labels.

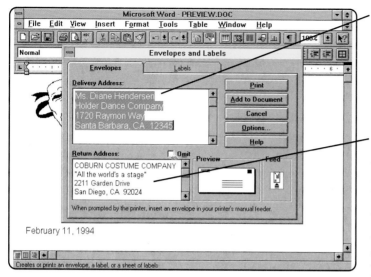

Notice that the address on your letter appears in the Delivery Address box. Word automatically searches for the address in the letter and enters it here.

Notice that the Return Address appears in the Return Address text box. This is the address typed in the User Info text box in the first section of this chapter entitled "Preparing an Envelope to Print."

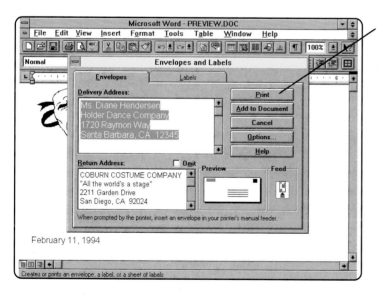

4. **Click** on **Print**. The Printing message box will appear.

If you change our mind, **click** on **Cancel**.

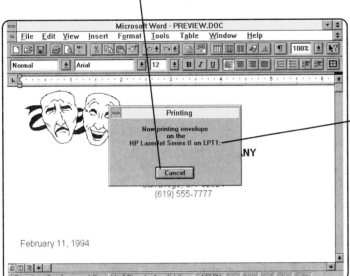

When the Print message box disappears, your printer will begin printing the envelope. Slick!

Notice that the name of your dot-matrix printer appears in this box.

You may have to fiddle with the position and alignment of your envelope in the printer to get it to print properly.

CUSTOMIZING THE RETURN ADDRESS

To make changes to Word's return address format, you must first attach the envelope to the document.

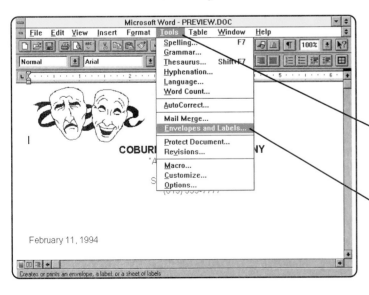

Attaching the Envelope to the Letter

1. Click on **Tools** in the menu bar. A pull-down menu will appear.

2. Click on **Envelopes and Labels**. The Envelopes and Labels dialog box will appear.

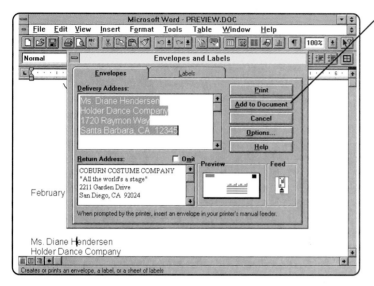

3. **Click** on **Add to Document**. The envelope will appear attached to the top of the first page of PREVIEW.DOC.

Changing the Envelope Style

1. **Click** in front of **COBURN** to set the cursor.

2. **Press and hold** the mouse button as you **drag** the mouse down to highlight the **return address**. **Release** the mouse button when the address is highlighted.

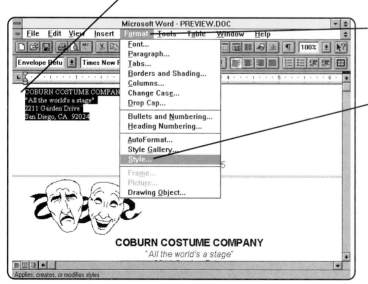

3. **Click** on **Format** in the menu bar. A pull-down menu will appear.

4. **Click** on **Style**. The Style dialog box will appear.

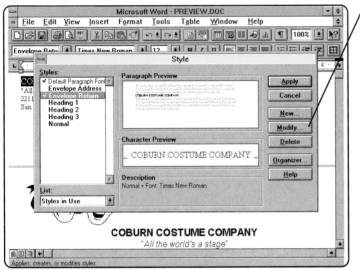

5. Click on **Modify**. The Modify Style dialog box will appear.

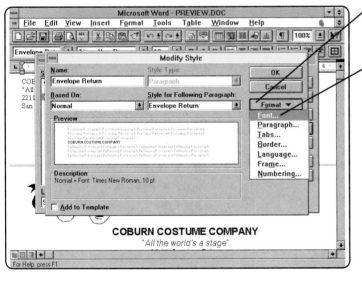

6. Click on **Format**. A drop-down list will appear.

7. Click on **Font**. The Font dialog box will appear.

8. Click on the ⬇ to the right of the Size text box to scroll down the list.

9. Click on **12**.

10. Click on **OK**. The Modify Style dialog box will appear.

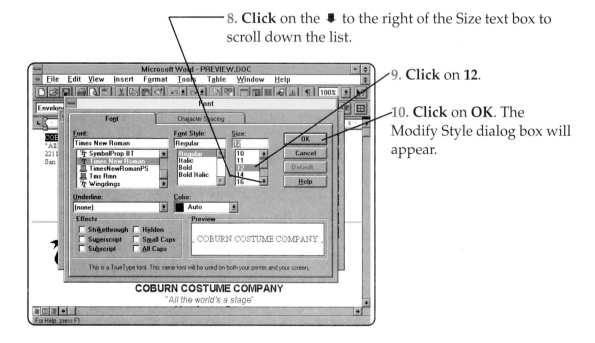

11. Click on **OK**. The Style dialog box will appear.

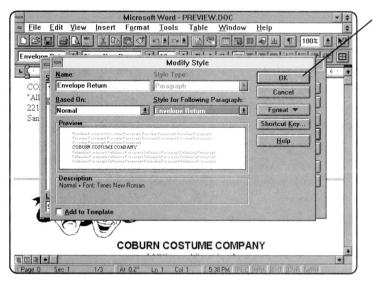

Notice that Envelope Return is highlighted in the Styles box.

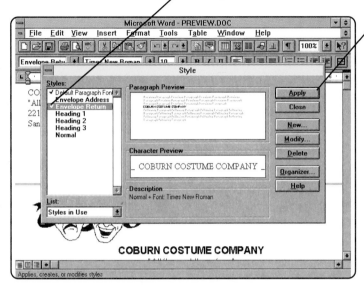

12. Click on **Apply**. PREVIEW.DOC will appear.

The Envelope Return style has now been applied to the return address. The style Times New Roman, 12 pt. is now the permanent style for envelope return addresses unless you change it.

Making the First Line of the Address Bold

1. Place the cursor to the **left** of **"COBURN"** and **click** to set the cursor.

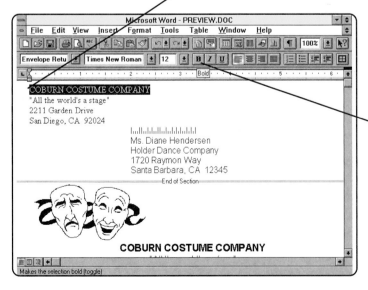

2. Press and hold the mouse button as you **drag** the cursor to highlight the company name.

3. Click on the **Bold button**. The highlighted text will change to bold.

4. Click anywhere off the text to remove the highlighting.

PRINTING THE LETTER AND THE ATTACHED ENVELOPE

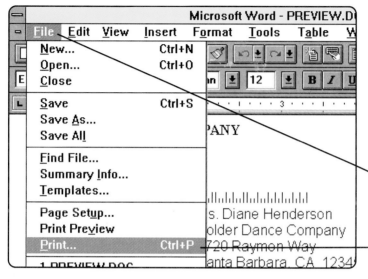

When you print with the Print button, the envelope will automatically be printed first, followed by the letter. If you want to print only the letter or only the envelope, go to the sections that follow this one.

1. **Click** on **File** in the menu bar. A pull-down menu will appear.

2 **Click** on **Print**. The Print dialog box will appear.

3. **Click** on **All** to place a black dot in the circle if the dot is not already there. The cursor will flash in the Copies box.

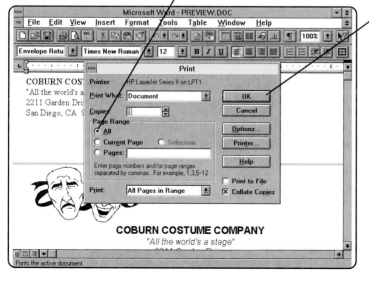

4. **Click** on **OK**. The Print message box will appear.

PRINTING THE ATTACHED ENVELOPE WITHOUT THE LETTER

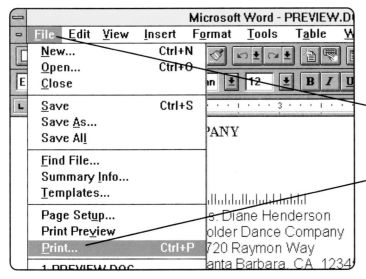

When you attach an envelope to a Word document, the envelope becomes page "0" of the document.

1. Click on **File** in the menu bar. A pull-down menu will appear.

2. Click on **Print**. The Print dialog box will appear.

3. Click on **Pages** to put a black dot in the circle. The cursor will flash in the Pages box.

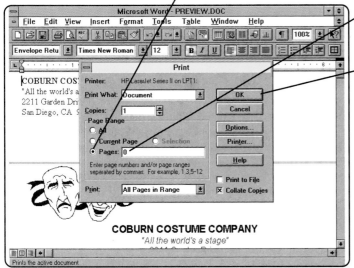

4. Type a **0** (zero) in the Pages box.

5. Click on **OK**. The Printing message box will appear. Only the attached envelope will be printed.

PRINTING THE LETTER WITHOUT THE ATTACHED ENVELOPE

1. **Click** on **File** in the menu bar. A pull-down menu will appear.

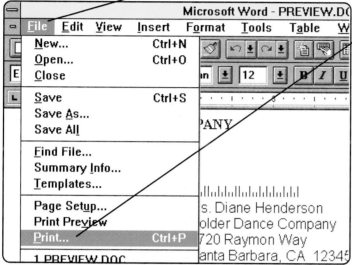

2. **Click** on **Print**. The Print dialog box will appear.

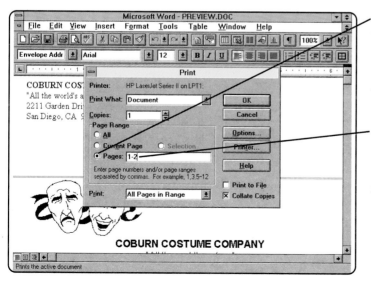

3. **Click** on **Pages** to place a black dot in the circle if the dot is not already there. The cursor will flash in the From box.

4. **Type 1-2** in the Page box.

5. **Click** on **OK**. The Printing message box will appear.

CLOSING WITHOUT SAVING THE ATTACHED ENVELOPE

1. **Click** on the **Control Menu box** (⊟) to the left of the title bar. A pull-down menu will appear.

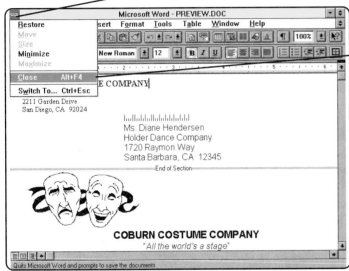

2. **Click** on **Close**. A Microsoft Word dialog box will appear.

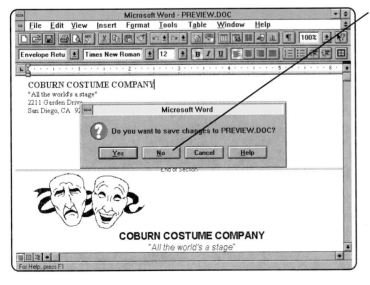

3. **Click** on **No**. The letter will close and the envelope will not be attached when you reopen the letter in later chapters.

Creating a Mailing List

With Word's mail merge feature, you can send the same letter (a form letter, for example) to different people and have the individual's name, address, salutation, and other information personalized on each letter without having to retype each letter. After you've written the letter, begin the print merge process by creating a mailing list, as shown in this chapter. Next you attach the mailing list to the letter and then code and merge print the letter with the mailing list (Chapters 14 and 15).

Even if you have a mailing list already created in another non-Windows (DOS-based) word processing program, such as WordPerfect or WordStar, work through this chapter and Chapters 14 and 15 to learn how Word's Merge Print features work. In this chapter you will do the following:

❖ Create a mailing list table of names and addresses, called a Data Source

OPENING A NEW
DATA SOURCE TABLE

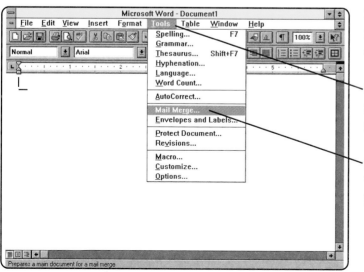

1. **Open** a new document file if one is not already open.

2. **Click** on **Tools** in the menu bar. A pull-down menu will appear.

3. **Click** on **Mail Merge**. The Merge Helper dialog box will appear.

4. Click on **Create**. A pull-down menu will appear.

5. Click on **Form Letters**. A Microsoft Word dialog box will appear.

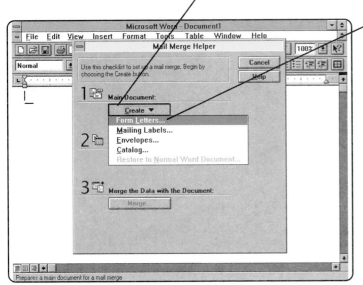

6. Click on **Active Window**. The Mail Merge Helper dialog box will appear.

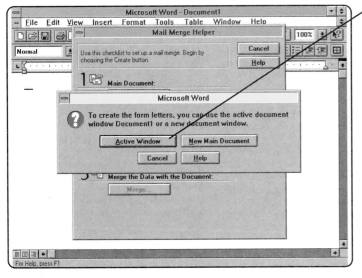

7. **Click** on **Get Data**. A pull-down menu will appear.

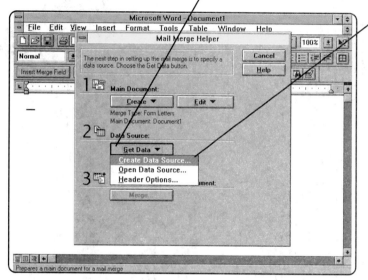

8. **Click** on **Create Data Source**. The Data Source dialog box will appear.

Setting Up the Header Row

To make sure that your mailing list prints properly, it helps to set it up in a table of rows and columns. The first row, called the *header row*, tells the computer what information is contained in each column by naming the fields for each column. A typical mailing list header row would consist of one row of *field names* (e.g. City, State, etc.), with the fields separated by table cells. Here's a typical header row:

FirstName	LastName	Street	City	State	Zip

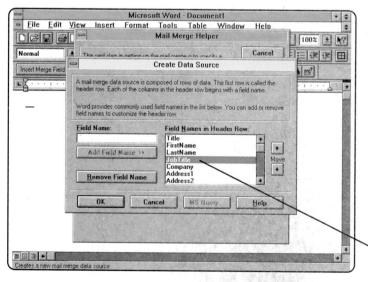

Removing Extra Field Names

Word provides you with a built-in list of field names. You can accept, rename, delete, or add to the list of field names to customize your mailing list.

1. **Click** on **Job Title** to highlight it.

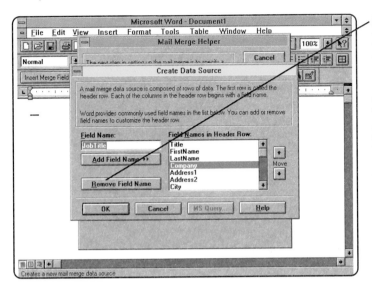

2. **Click** on **Remove Field Name**. Job Title will move to the Field Name text box.

3. **Press** the **Delete key**. Job Title will disappear. The Field Name text box will be blank with the cursor flashing in it.

Adding a New Field Name

Word's built-in field name list may not contain the field names you want in your mailing list. You can add field names in this section.

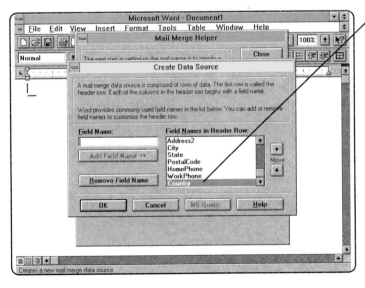

1. **Click** on **Country** to highlight it.

2. **Click** on **Remove Field Name**. Country will move to the Field Name text box.

3. **Press** the **Delete Key**. Country will disappear. The Field Name text box will be blank with the cursor flashing in it.

4. Type Greeting.

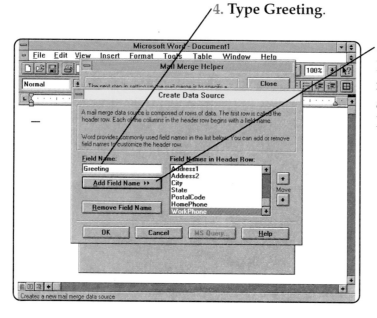

5. Click on **Add Field Name**. The new header field name, Greeting, will be added to the bottom of the Field Name list box.

Notice that Greeting is now at the bottom of the Field Name list.

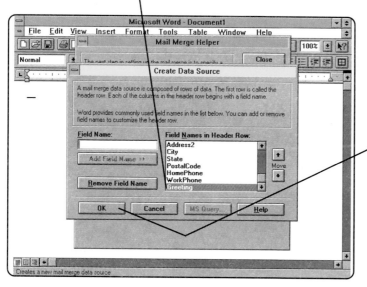

SAVING THE DATA SOURCE FILE

1. Click on **OK**. The Save Data Source dialog box will appear.

2. Type mylist (Word will automatically add the .doc extension).

3. Click on **OK**. A Microsoft Word dialog box will appear.

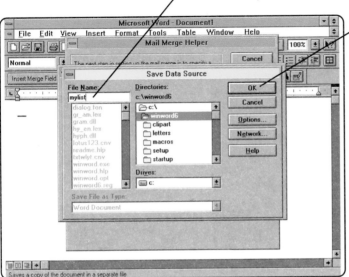

ENTERING NAMES AND ADDRESSES IN THE DATA SOURCE TABLE

1. Click on **Edit Data Source**. The Data Form dialog box will appear.

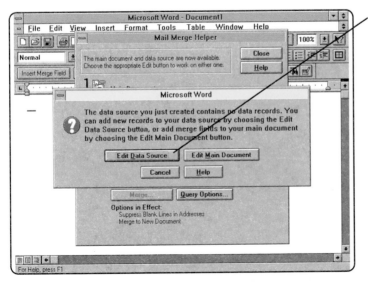

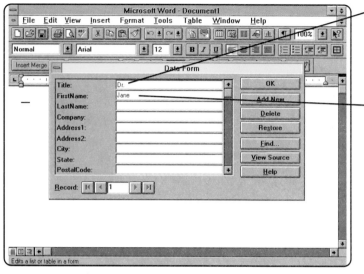

2. Type Dr. and **press** the **Tab key**. The cursor will move to the FirstName text box.

3. Type Jane and **press** the **Tab key**. The cursor will move to the LastName text box.

4. Repeat step 2 to type the following information in the data entry text boxes:

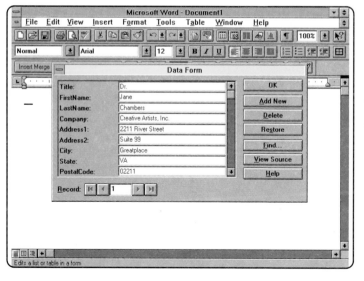

Chambers

Creative Artists, Inc.

2211 River Street

Suite 99

Greatplace

VA

02211

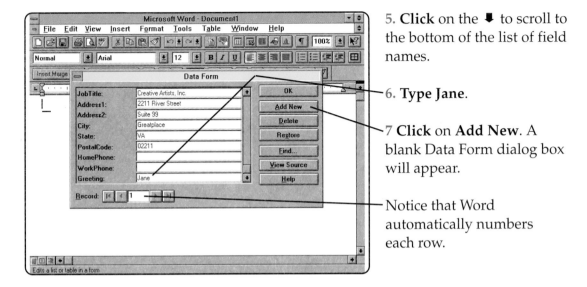

5. Click on the ⬇ to scroll to the bottom of the list of field names.

6. Type Jane.

7 Click on **Add New**. A blank Data Form dialog box will appear.

Notice that Word automatically numbers each row.

8. Repeat steps 2 to 4 above to type the following information:

Mr.

James

Avery

North Carolina Entertainment, Ltd.

32234 Tar Heel Drive

Building 21147

Plantation

NC

01934

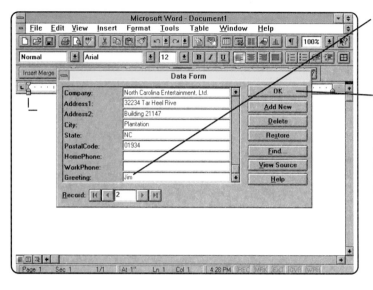

9. Repeat steps 5 to 6 to type Jim in the Greeting text box.

10. Click on **OK**. The empty form letter document that you began this process with will appear. The Mail Merge toolbar will appear on the document screen.

VIEWING THE DATA SOURCE

Notice that the Mail Merge toolbar has automatically appeared.

You have just set up a Data Source table for your mailing list, entered the names and addresses of two people and what do you see? A blank document screen with a new toolbar! Strange. Just hang in there. These next steps will show you exactly what you have accomplished.

1. Click on **Tools** in the menu bar. A pull-down menu will appear.

2. Click on **Mail Merge**. The Mail Merge Helper dialog box will appear.

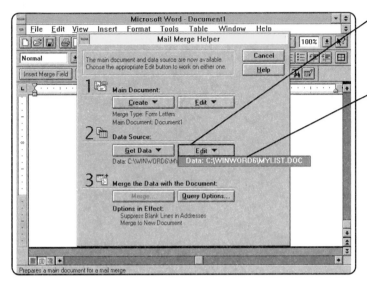

3. Click on **Edit**. A drop-down list of data source files will appear.

4. Click on **Data: C:\WINWORD6\ MYLIST.DOC**. The Data Form dialog box will appear.

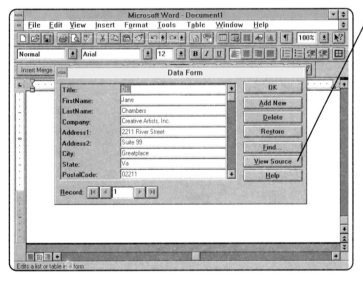

5. Click on **View Source**. Voila! At long last the data source table you created, along with the addresses you entered, will appear!

Improving the View

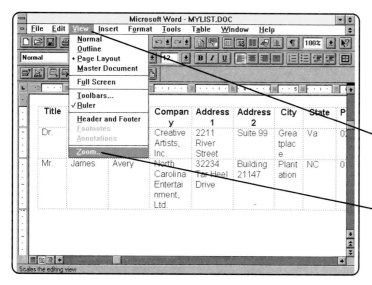

Don't panic. The table looks weird but it isn't your fault! In this section, you can fix the view with just a few mouse clicks.

1. Click on **View** in the menu bar. A pull-down menu will appear.

2. Click on **Zoom**. The Zoom dialog box will appear.

3. Click on **Page Width**.

4. Click on **OK**.

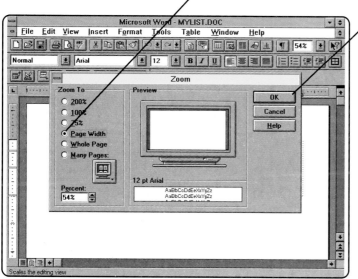

CLOSING WORD

1. Click twice on the **Control Menu box** on the title bar. A Microsoft Word dialog box will appear.

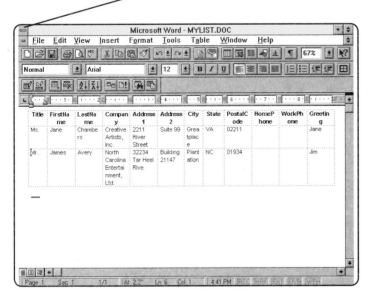

2. Click on **No**. The Program Manager window will appear.

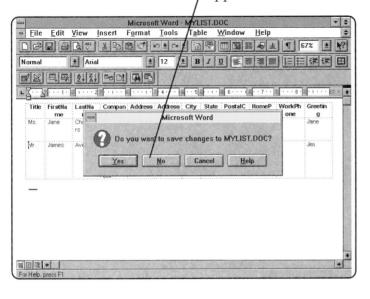

Note: In Word you cannot create a data source table or use the mail merge toolbar unless that data source table is attached to a document. In this example, Document1 was used strictly for the purpose of creating the data source table, mylist.doc. Therefore, you do not need to save it now that the mylist.doc has been created and saved.

Setting Up and Merge Printing a Form Letter

In Chapter 13 you completed your mailing list by adding new fields and data. You are now ready to code the letter to match the mailing list so that it will print personalized letters correctly. In this chapter you will do the following:

❖ Code a form letter
❖ Merge print the form letter

ATTACHING A MAILING LIST FILE TO A LETTER

1. Open PREVIEW.DOC if it is not already on your screen.

2. Click on **Tools**. A pull-down menu will appear.

3. Click on **Mail Merge**. The Mail Merge Helper screen will appear.

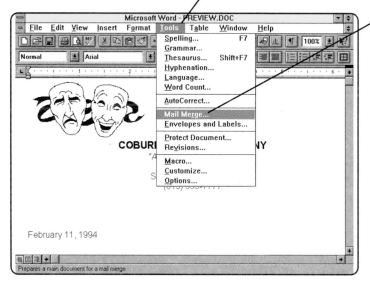

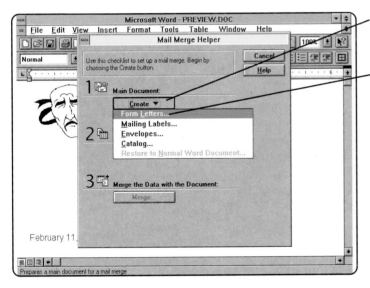

4. Click on **Create**. A drop-down list will appear.

5. Click on **Form Letters**. The Microsoft Word dialog box will appear.

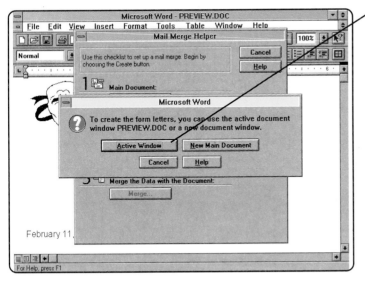

6. Click on **Active Window**. The Mail Merge Helper dialog box will appear.

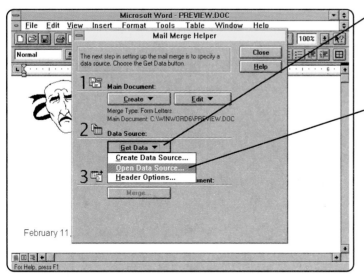

7. **Click** on **Get Data** in the Data Source text box. A drop-down menu will appear.

8. **Click** on **Open Date Source**. The Open Data Source dialog box will appear.

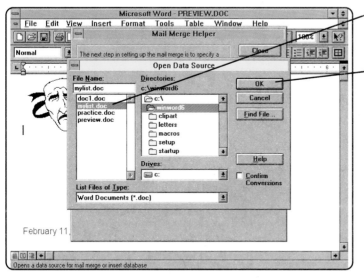

9. **Click** on **mylist.doc** in the Filename text box.

10. **Click** on **OK**. A Microsoft Word dialog box will appear.

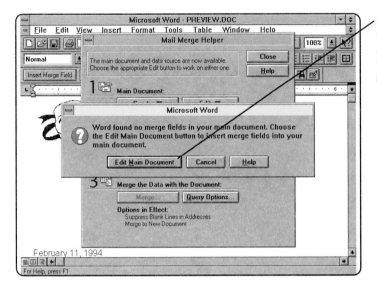

11. Click on **Edit Main Document**. The PREVIEW.DOC document screen will appear.

INSERTING MERGE FIELDS INTO A FORM LETTER

1. Move the mouse pointer to the **left** of **"Ms."**

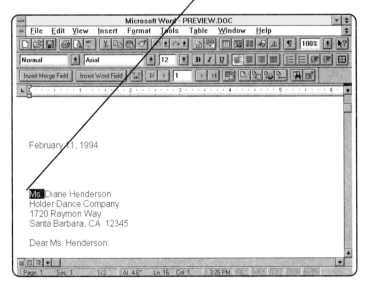

2. Press and hold the mouse button as you **drag** to the right to highlight **"Ms."**

3. Release the mouse button.

4. Click on **Insert Merge Field**. A pull-down menu will appear.

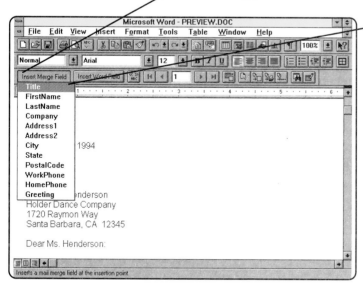

5. Click on **Title**. The "Ms." prefix will be replaced with the merge field <<Title>>. This means that when you print the form letter, the title (Dr., Mrs., Mr., etc.) will be inserted in the letter for each person on the list.

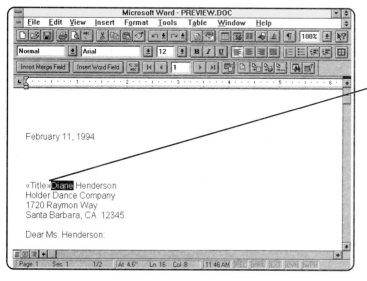

Do not place a space between the field <<Title>> and "Diane."

6. Move the mouse pointer to the **left** of **"Diane."**

7. Press and hold the mouse button as you **drag** to the **right** to highlight **"Diane"** and **release** the mouse button.

8. **Click** on **Insert Merge Field**. A pull-down menu will appear.

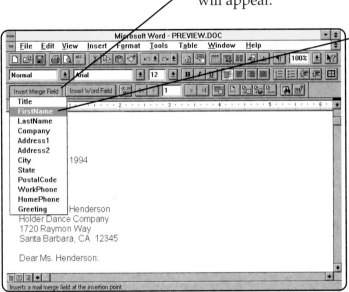

9. **Click** on **FirstName**. "Diane" will be replaced with the merge field <<FirstName>>. This means that when you print the form letter, the first name of each person in your mailing list will be inserted in the letter printed for that person.

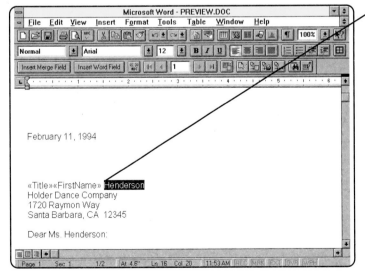

10. **Move** the mouse pointer to the **left** of **"Henderson."**

11. **Press and hold** the mouse button as you **drag** to the **right** to highlight **"Henderson."**

12. **Release** the mouse button.

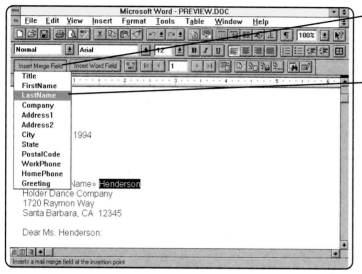

13. Click on **Insert Merge Field**. A pull-down menu will appear.

14. Click on **LastName**. "Henderson" will be replaced with the merge field <<LastName>>. (Remember to put a space between the merge fields.) This means that when you print the form letter, the last name of each person in your mailing list will be inserted in the letter printed for that person.

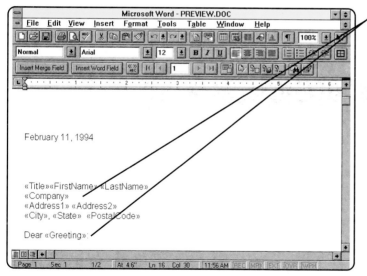

15. Repeat steps 10 through 14 to insert the other merge field codes into the remaining address and salutation sections of the form letter. Make certain you do not highlight the comma after "Santa Barbara" or the colon after "Henderson." Be sure to highlight both "Ms." and "Henderson" and replace them with the merge field "Greeting." Add <<Address2>> merge field to the street address line to allow for suite numbers in your mailing list.

If you goof and put a merge field in the wrong place, highlight it and repeat steps 10 through 14 to replace it with the correct merge field. Be careful not to add or delete spaces.

Inserting Personalized Information into the Body of the Letter

Just as you've personalized the letter by adding a name, address, and greeting to the first page of the letter, you can also insert personal touches in the body of the letter using the same kind of fields used on page 1 of the letter.

1. Click on the **button** on the scroll bar and hold as you move the button approximately halfway down the scroll bar to bring the bottom of page 1 into view.

2. Repeat steps 2 through 5 in the previous section "Inserting Merge Fields into a Form Letter" to insert the <<Title>> merge field.

3. Repeat steps 6 through 9 in the same section to insert the <<LastName>> merge field.

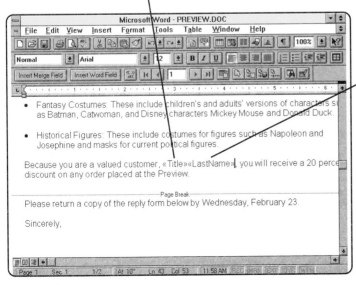

Inserting Personalized Information into the Header

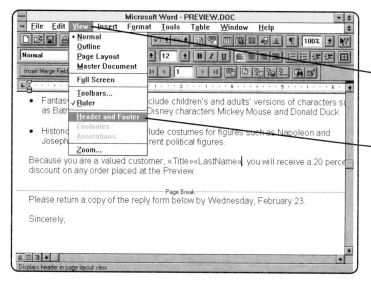

You can individualize the headers of a letter.

1. Click on **View** in the menu bar. A pull-down menu will appear.

2. Click on **Header and Footer.** The Header and Footer toolbar will appear.

3. Repeat steps 1 through 5 in the section entitled "Inserting Merge Fields into a Form Letter" to insert the <<Title>> merge field.

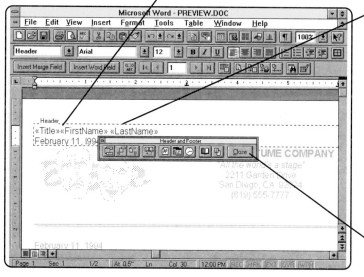

4. Repeat steps 6 through 9 in the same section to insert the <<FirstName>> and <<LastName>> merge fields.

Remember not to space between the <<Title>> and <<FirstName>> field and press the Enter key after the <<LastName>> field.

5. Click on **Close.** PREVIEW.DOC will appear.

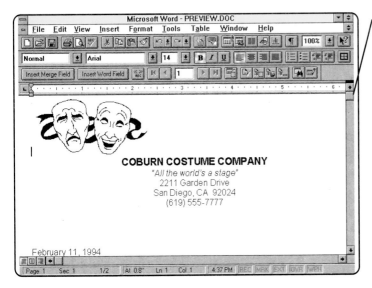

6. Click on the **button** on the scroll bar and hold as you move the button approximately three-fourths of the way down the scroll bar to bring page 2 into view.

7. Repeat steps 1 through 9 in the section entitled "Inserting Merge Fields into a Form Letter" once again to insert the merge field codes into the reply form on page 2.

PRINTING THE FORM LETTER

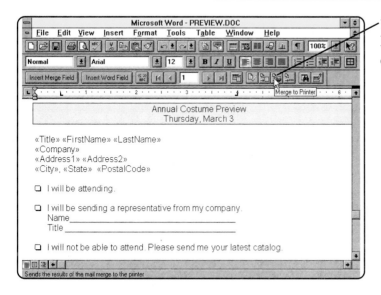

1. **Click** on the **Merge to Printer button**. The Print dialog box will appear.

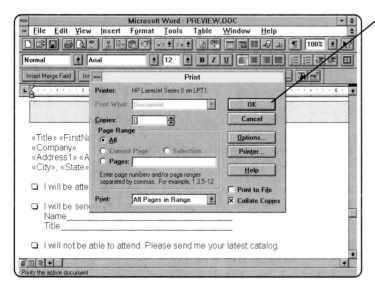

2. **Click** on **OK**. A Printing message dialog box will appear.

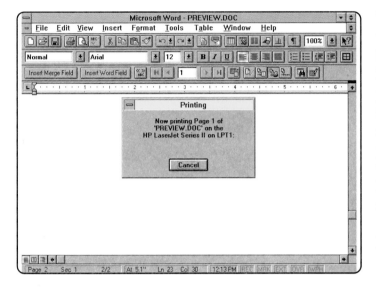

The Printing message box will stay on the screen until both pages of the document have been sent to the printer. Your printer will now print two, two-page form letters using the personalized information that you entered into the MYLIST.DOC mailing list file.

Isn't this great?

SAVING YOUR FORM LETTER

1. **Click** on **File** in the menu bar.

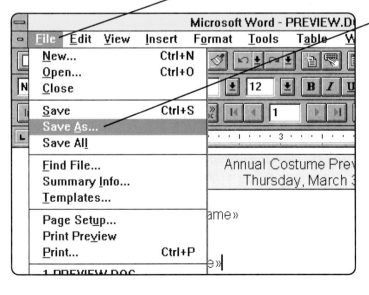

2. **Click** on **Save As**. The Save As dialog box will appear.

3. Type myform in the File Name box.

4. Click on **OK**. MYFORM.DOC will appear in the title bar.

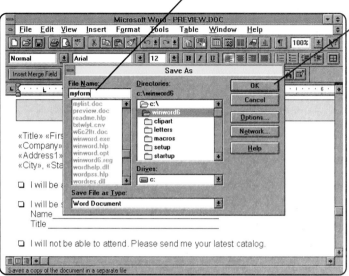

Closing the Form Letter

1. Click on the **Control Menu box** (☐) to the left of the menu bar. A pull-down menu will appear.

2. Click on **Close**. A Microsoft Word dialog box will appear.

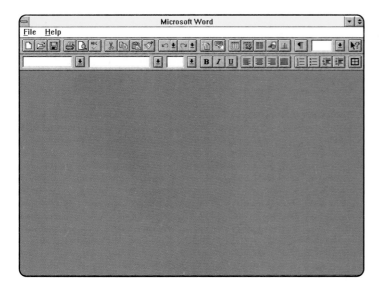

You will be returned to a blank Word screen.

Merge Printing Envelopes for a Mailing List

You can print envelopes from any mailing list totally separate from any form letter connected to the mailing list. You do this by creating and saving a merge printing envelope document set up to print from a specific mailing list. We recommend that you do this chapter only if you have an envelope feeder for a laser jet printer or tractor feed envelopes. In this chapter you will do the following:

❖ Create an envelope document file for printing envelopes from a mailing list

❖ Print envelopes from a mailing list

❖ Print a specific envelope from a mailing list

CREATING AN ENVELOPE DOCUMENT FILE FOR A MAILING LIST

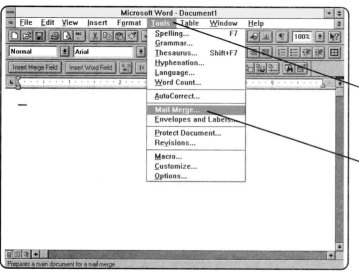

1. **Open** a new document if one isn't already on your screen.

2. **Click** on **Tools** in the menu bar. A pull-down menu will appear.

3. **Click** on **Mail Merge**. The Mail Merge Helper dialog box will appear.

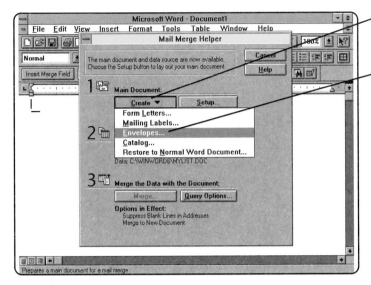

4. Click on **Create**. A drop-down list will appear.

5. Click on **Envelopes**. A Microsoft Word dialog box will appear.

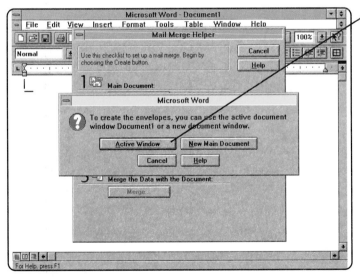

6. Click on **Active Window**. The Merge Helper dialog box will appear.

7. Click on **Get Data**. A drop-down list will appear.

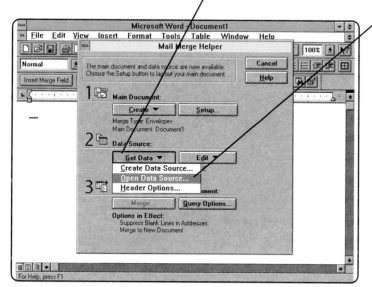

8. Click on **Open Data Source**. The Open Data Source dialog box will appear.

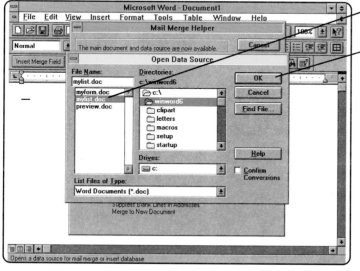

9. Click on **mylist.doc**.

10. Click on **OK**. A Microsoft dialog box will appear.

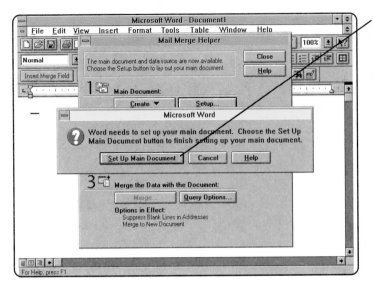

11. **Click** on **Set Up Main Document**. The Envelopes Option dialog box will appear.

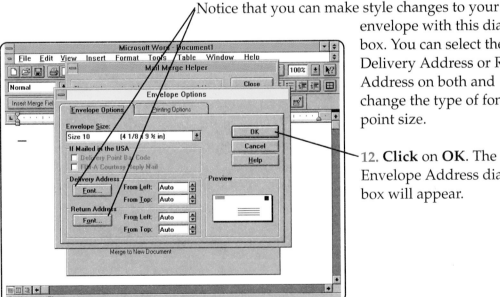

Notice that you can make style changes to your envelope with this dialog box. You can select the Delivery Address or Return Address on both and change the type of font and point size.

12. **Click** on **OK**. The Envelope Address dialog box will appear.

INSERTING MERGE FIELD NAMES INTO THE ENVELOPE

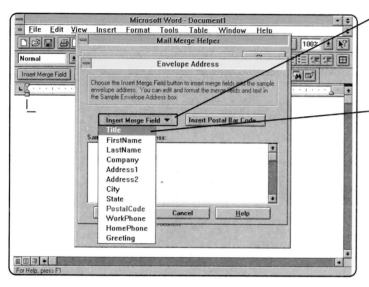

1. Click on **Insert Merge Field**. A drop-down list of merge field names will appear.

2. Click on **Title**. <<Title>> will appear in the Sample Envelope Address dialog box.

3. Press the **Spacebar**.

4. Repeat steps 1 through 3 to place the <<FirstName>> and <<LastName>> field in the Sample Envelope Address text box.

5. Press the **Enter key**. The cursor will move to the next line of the address.

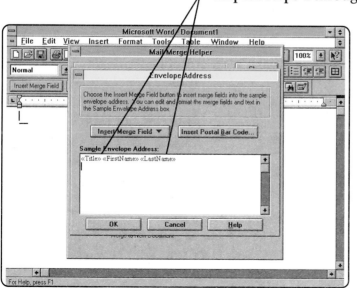

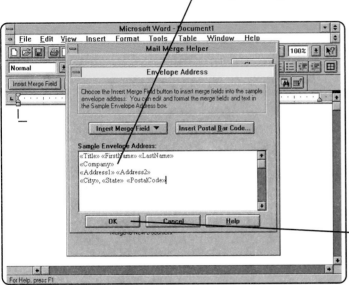

6. Repeat steps 1 to 3 in this section to insert the remaining merge fields in the Sample Envelope Address text box.

Press the **Enter key** at the end of each line. Insert a comma followed by a space after the <<City>> field. Put two spaces between the <<State>> and <<PostalCode>> field.

7. Click on **OK**. The Mail Merge Helper dialog box will appear.

MERGE PRINTING
THE ENTIRE MAILING LIST

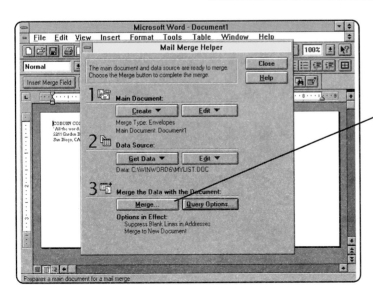

Insert an envelope tray in your laser printer (or put tractor feed envelopes in your dot-matrix printer).

1. Click on **Merge**. The Merge dialog box will appear.

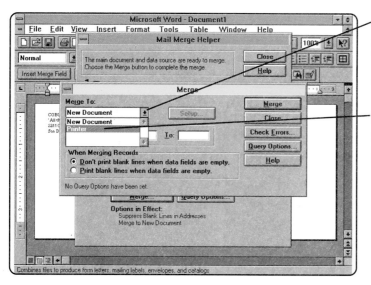

2. **Click** on the ⬇ to the right of the Merge To list box. A drop-down list will appear.

3. **Click** on **Printer**. It will appear in the Merge To text box.

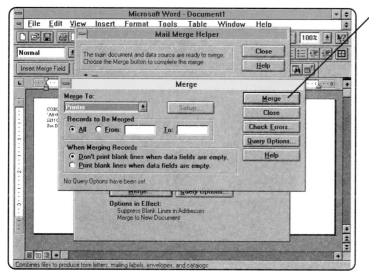

4. **Click** on **Merge**. The Mail Merge Helper dialog box will appear.

5. Click on **All** to place a black dot in the circle if the dot is not already there.

6. Click on **OK**. A Printing message box will appear.

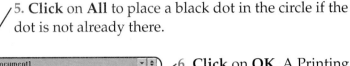

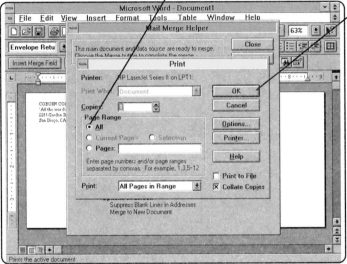

A Printing Message box will stay on the screen until the envelopes have been sent to the printer for printing.

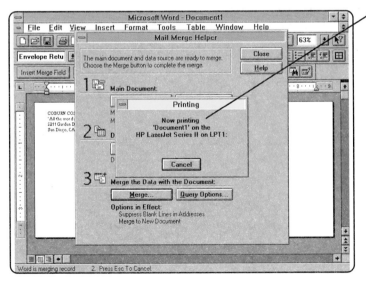

SAVING THE ENVELOPE

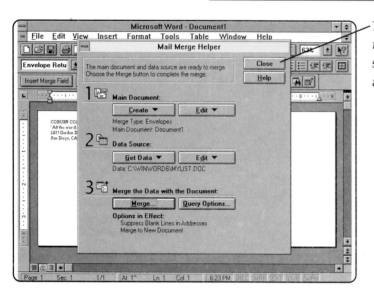

1. Click on **Close**. The *unsaved* merge envelope screen (Document 1) will appear.

2. Click on the **Save button** on the toolbar. The Save As dialog box will appear. The filename, doc1.doc, will be highlighted in the Filename text box.

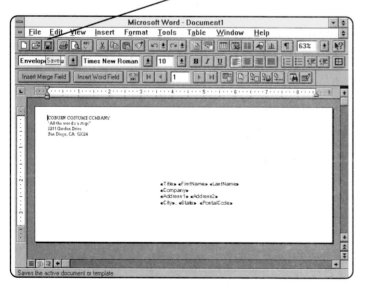

3. **Type myenv**.

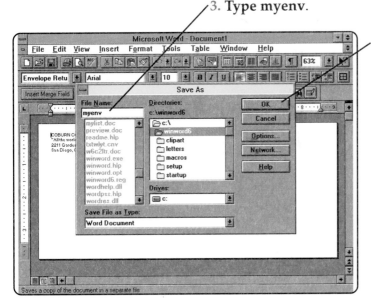

4. **Click** on **OK**. The MYENV.DOC window will appear.

PRINTING AN ENVELOPE FOR A SPECIFIC ADDRESS FROM A MAILING LIST

Most people have long mailing lists (not like the two addresses listed in the example in this chapter). If you want to print an envelope for a specific address from your list, you need to know the location of that address (row number) in the mailing list before you can merge print. Word makes it easy to search the list for a specific name, address, postal code, etc.

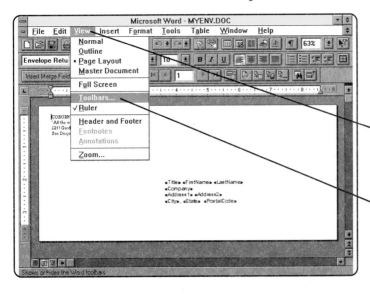

Finding a Specific Address

1. **Click** on **View** in the menu bar. A pull-down menu will appear.

2. **Click** on **Toolbars**. The Toolbars dialog box will appear.

3. Click on **Database** to place an ✕ in the box.

4. Click on **OK**.

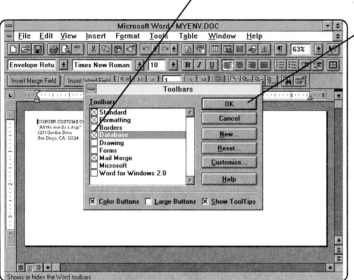

5. Click on the **Data Form tool** on the Databar toolbar. The Data Form dialog box will appear.

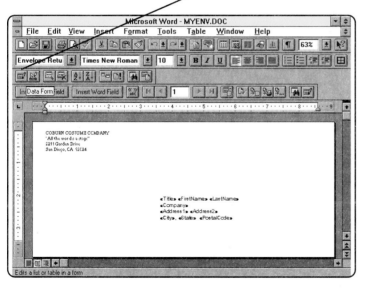

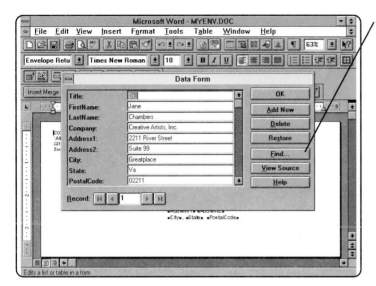

6. Click on **Find**. The Find In Field dialog box will appear.

7. **Type "Avery"** in the Find What text box.

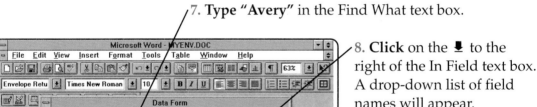

8. Click on the ⬇ to the right of the In Field text box. A drop-down list of field names will appear.

9. Click on **LastName**. It will appear in the In Field text box.

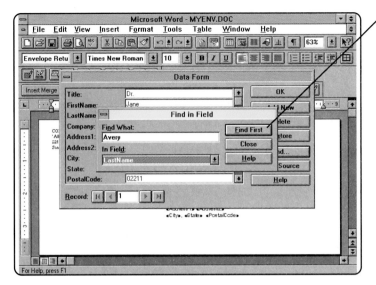

10. Click on **Find First**. Mr. Avery's record number will appear in the Record box.

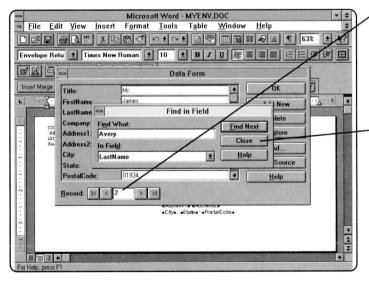

Notice Mr. Avery's record number is "2". You will need the record number to print an envelope just for him.

11. Click on **Close**. The Data Form dialog box will appear. Mr. Avery's record will be shown.

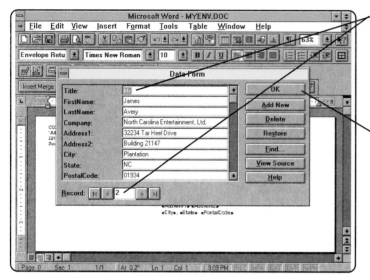

Notice that the Avery data information appears in the Data Form dialog box. The record number "2" appears in the Record box.

12. Click on **OK**. The MYENV.DOC window will appear.

MERGE PRINTING A SPECIFIC ENVELOPE

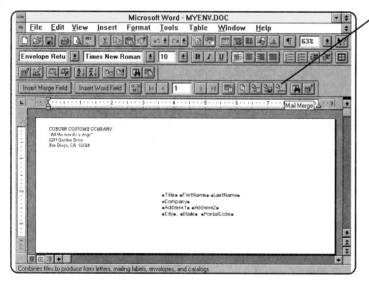

1. Click on the **Mail Merge button** on the Mail Merge toolbar. The Merge dialog box will appear.

2. **Click** on **From** to place a black dot in the circle. The cursor will be flashing in the From text box.

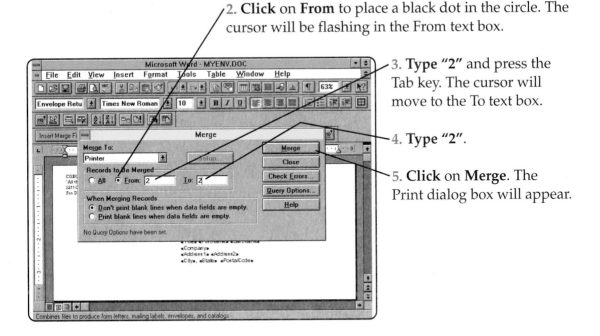

3. **Type "2"** and press the Tab key. The cursor will move to the To text box.

4. **Type "2"**.

5. **Click** on **Merge**. The Print dialog box will appear.

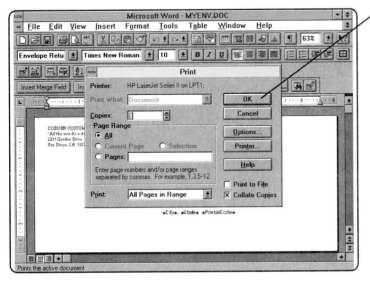

6. **Click** on **OK**. The Printing message box will appear briefly. The envelope will print and then the MYENV.DOC window will reappear.

REMOVING THE TOOL BAR

1. Click on **View** in the menu bar. A pull-down menu will appear.

2. Click on **Toolbar**. The Toolbars dialog box will appear.

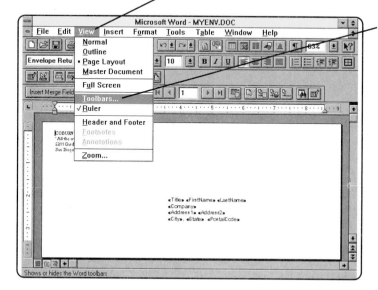

3. Click on **Database** to remove the X in the box.

4. Click on **OK**. MYENV.DOC will appear.

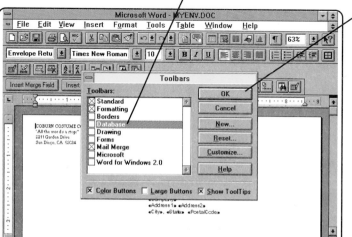

CLOSING WORD

1. Click on the **Normal View button** on the horizontal scroll bar at the bottom of the page. MYENV.DOC will appear in the standard view.

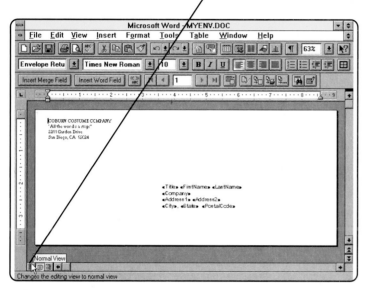

2. Click twice on the **Control Menu box**. A Microsoft Word dialog box will appear.

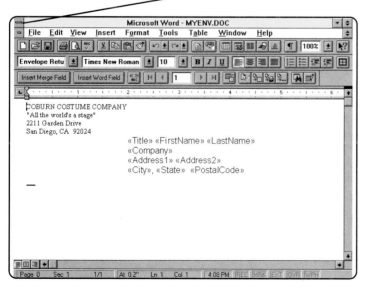

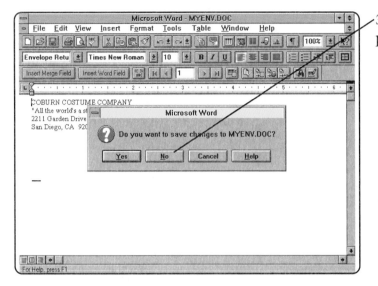

3. **Click** on **No**. The Word 6 program will close.

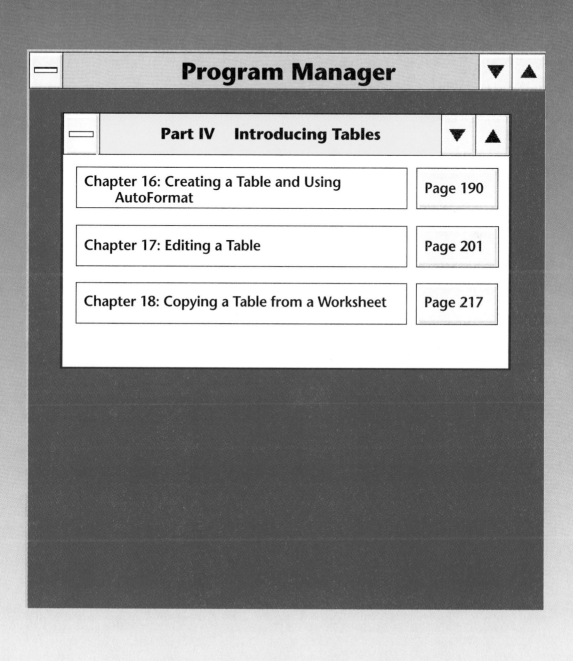

Program Manager

Part IV   Introducing Tables

Creating a Table and Using AutoFormat

The Tables feature in Word 6 makes it easy to organize information into columns and rows. You can join cells in the table to make room for a heading, increase the number of lines in a cell for a multiline entry, change the width of a column, and add and delete rows and columns with ease. You can also sort data on various criteria. Word has a selection of 34 different pre-designed formats which you can apply to your table to create visual interest. In this chapter you will do the following:

❖ Create a table

❖ Apply a pre-designed AutoFormat to the table

❖ Join cells

❖ Enter and format text and numbers

❖ Align text and numbers within the table

CREATING A TABLE

In this chapter you will create a table with four columns and six rows. You can insert a table anywhere in an existing document. In this example, however, you will open a new document for the table if you do not already have a blank document on your screen.

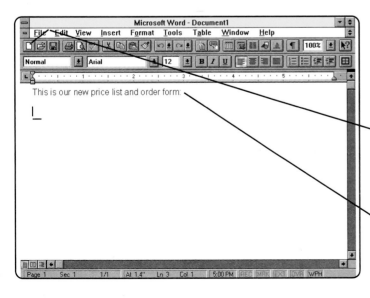

1. Click on the **New Document button** on the toolbar. A blank document will appear on your screen.

2. Type the sentence **This is our new price list and order form.** Then **press Enter twice**.

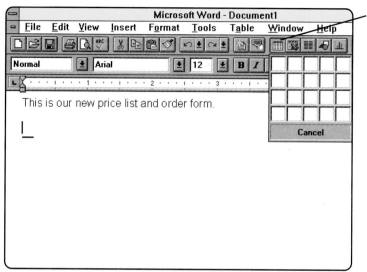

3. **Click** on the **Table button** on the toolbar. A table grid will appear.

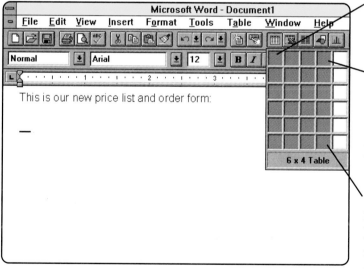

4. **Click and hold** on the **first square** of the table grid.

5. **Continue to hold** the mouse button and **drag** the highlight bar **across four squares**. This tells Word to put four columns in the table.

6. **Continue to hold** the mouse button and **drag** the highlight bar **down six rows**. The grid will add two rows as you drag.

7. **Release** the mouse button. A six-row by four-column table will appear.

You can also create a table by clicking on Table in the menu bar then clicking on Insert Table on the pull-down menu. But it's not nearly as much fun as using the Table button.

Notice the column indicators in the ruler bar.

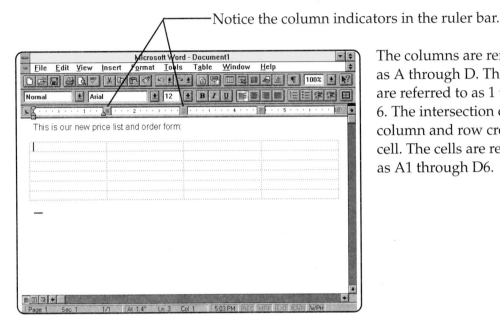

The columns are referred to as A through D. The rows are referred to as 1 through 6. The intersection of each column and row creates a cell. The cells are referred to as A1 through D6.

USING TABLE AUTOFORMAT

Word has 34 pre-designed formats that you can apply to your table to give it a polished look.

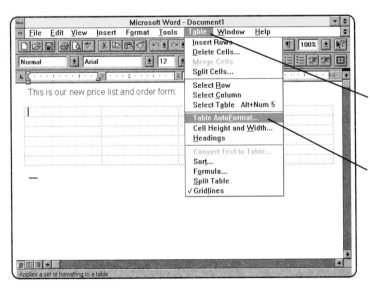

1. **Click** in the **first row** of the table to place the cursor if it is not already there.

2. **Click** on **Table** in the menu bar. A pull-down menu will appear.

3. **Click** on **Table AutoFormat**. The Table AutoFormat dialog box will appear.

Notice that the choice highlighted in the Formats list box is shown in the Preview box on the right.

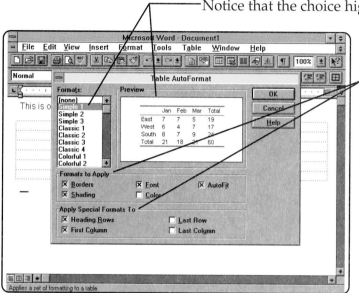

Notice also that you can choose which features of the style you want by clicking the X in each box on or off.

4. Click on the ⬇ on the scroll bar to scroll through the list of formatting choices.

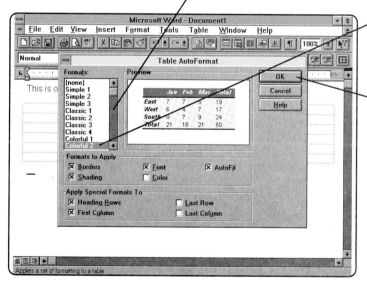

5. Click on **Colorful 2** when you have finished viewing all the choices.

6. Click on **OK**. The dialog box will close and the table will appear with the Colorful 2 formatting.

MERGING CELLS

When you merge cells, you remove the dividing lines between them to create a single, larger cell. In this section you will merge cells in the first row to create a single cell for a two-line heading.

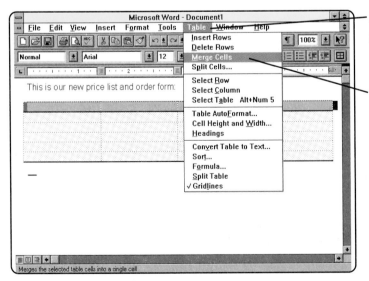

1. Click in the left margin beside the first row. The entire row will be highlighted.

2. Click on **Table** in the menu bar. A pull-down menu will appear.

3. Click on **Merge Cells**. The dividing lines will be removed from the cells in the first row.

4. Click anywhere on the document to remove the highlighting and see the change.

ENTERING TEXT AND NUMBERS IN A TABLE

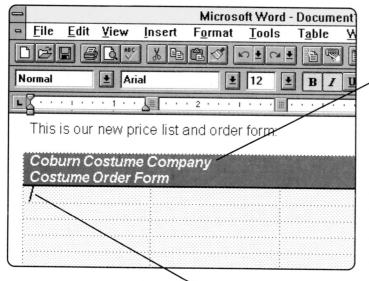

You enter and edit text in a table just as you do in the document itself.

1. Click on the **first row** in the table (Cell A1) if your cursor is not already there. **Type Coburn Costume Company**.

2. Press Enter. This will add a line to the cell you are in.

3. Type Costume Order Form.

4. Press the **Tab key** on your keyboard. This will move you to the next cell, A2.

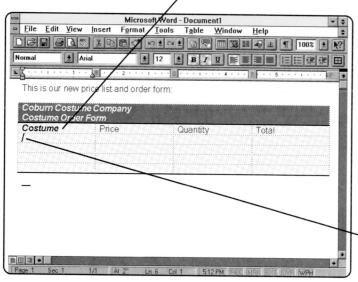

5. Type Costume and **press** the **Tab key**. The cursor will move to the next cell (B2). If you accidentally press Enter, an extra line will be added to the cell. Simply press the Backspace key and the extra line will be deleted.

6. Type Price and **press Tab** to move to the next cell.

7. Type Quantity and **press Tab**. The cursor will move to the next cell.

8. Type Total and **press Tab**. The cursor will move to the first cell in the next row.

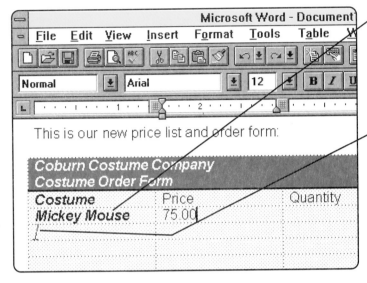

9. **Type Mickey Mouse** in C1 and **press Tab** to move the cursor to the next cell.

10. **Type 75.00**.

11. **Place** the mouse pointer in the blank **cell below Mickey Mouse** in about ⅛ inch inside the cell. It will become an I-beam.

12. **Click** to set the cursor in place.

When you're in a table, the cursor changes shape with annoying speed. You may have to fiddle with the placement until it is the shape you want.

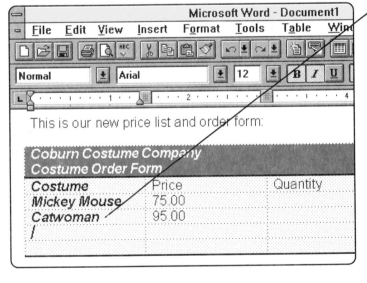

13. **Type Catwoman** and **press Tab** to move to the next cell.

14. **Type 95.00**.

15. **Click** in the blank cell **below Catwoman**. (Remember that your cursor should be in the shape of an I-beam when you click in the cell.)

16. Type **Phantom Mask** and **press Tab** to move to the next cell.

17. Type 9.95.

18. Click in the blank cell **below Phantom Mask** to place the cursor.

(You can move through the table with the Tab key, the arrow keys on your keyboard, or simply by clicking on the cell you want.)

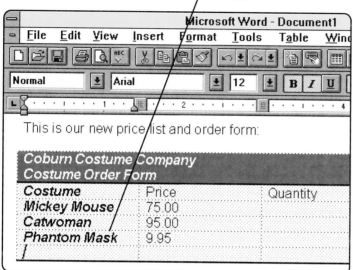

19. Click on **A6** and **type Totals**.

CENTERING TEXT IN A TABLE

You format the data in a table the same way you format it in the document itself. First, you highlight the text you want to format.

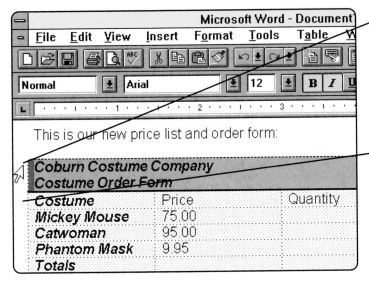

1. **Click** in the left margin beside **Coburn Costume Company**. The entire line will be highlighted. (The mouse pointer should be in the shape of an arrow.)

2. **Press and hold** the mouse button and **drag** the arrow down to Costume. All three lines of type will be highlighted.

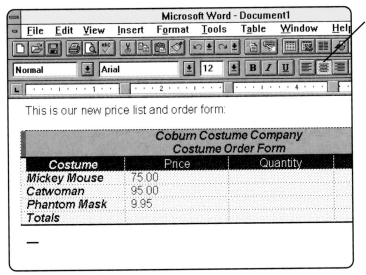

3. **Click** on the **Center button** on the toolbar. The highlighted text will be centered in each cell.

4. **Click anywhere** to remove the highlighting.

ALIGNING NUMBERS IN A TABLE

In this example you will align the numbers in column B to the right of the cell on the decimal point.

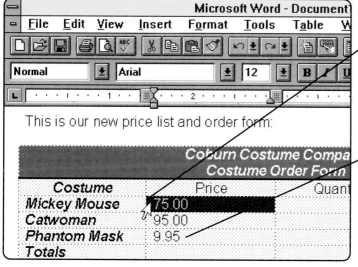

1. Place the mouse pointer in B3 **just to the left of 75**. It should be in the shape of a right-pointing arrow. **Click** to highlight the cell.

2. Click and hold the mouse button and **drag** the arrow down to 9.95 in B5. All three cells in column B will be highlighted.

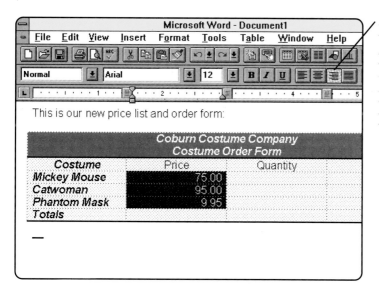

3. Click on the **Align Right button** on the toolbar. The highlighted text will move to the right of the cell and line up on the decimal point.

SAVING THE TABLE

1. **Click** on the **Save button** on the toolbar. The Save As dialog box will appear.

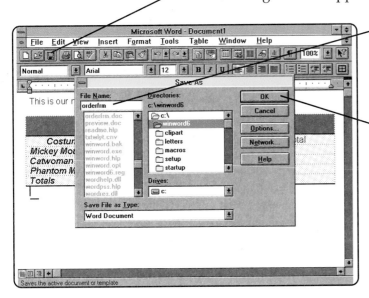

2. **Type orderfrm**. It will replace the highlighted doc1.doc that appears in the File Name box.

3. **Click** on **OK**. The dialog box will close and the table will be saved.

Editing a Table

You'll love the ease with which you can edit the contents of a table as well as change the structure of the table itself. You can sort data in a table (or in a letter) alphabetically and numerically. You can add and delete rows and columns with ease. You can also print a table with or without grid lines. In this chapter you will do the following:

❖ Sort data alphabetically on the first cell in a row
❖ Sort data numerically on the second cell in a row
❖ Add and delete a row and a column
❖ Change column width
❖ Change the position of a table so that it is centered across the page
❖ Print a table with or without grid lines
❖ Delete a table
❖ Undo and redo multiple steps

SORTING DATA ALPHABETICALLY

You can sort data in a document and in a table. In this example you will sort the data in rows 3 through 5 alphabetically by the first cell in each row. Because you do not want to sort the entire table, you will highlight the rows you want to sort.

Microsoft Word - ORDERFRM.

File Edit View Insert Format Tools Table W

Normal   Arial   12   B I

This is our new price list and order form:

	Coburn Costume Compa	
	Costume Order Form	
Costume	Price	Quant
Mickey Mouse	75.00	
Catwoman	95.00	
Phantom Mask	9.95	
Totals		

1. **Click** outside the table beside **Mickey Mouse**. The pointer will be in the shape of an arrow. The entire row will be highlighted.

2. **Press and hold** the mouse button and **drag** the arrow down to the **end** of the **Phantom Mask row**. All three rows will be highlighted.

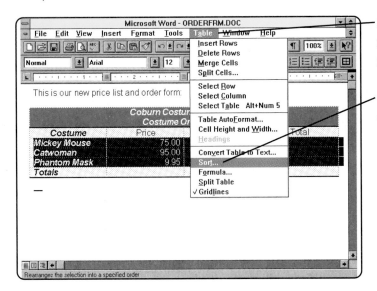

3. Click on **Table** in the menu bar. A pull-down menu will appear.

4. Click on **Sort**. The Sort dialog box will appear.

5. Confirm that **Column 1** is in the Sort By box. This means that the data will be sorted on the first cell in the row.

6. Confirm that **Text** is in the Type box. This means that data will be sorted alphabetically.

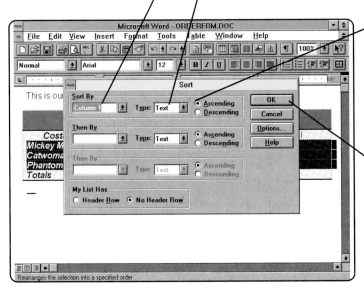

7. Click on **Ascending** to put a dot in the circle if one is not already there. *Ascending* means the sort will be in A to Z (or 1 to n) order.

8. Click on **OK**. The dialog box will close and the highlighted lines will be sorted alphabetically based on the first cell in each row.

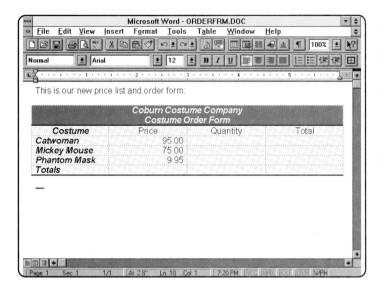

9. **Click anywhere** on the document to remove the highlighting.

Your screen will look like this.

Pretty neat!

SORTING DATA NUMERICALLY

In this example you will sort the data in rows 3 through 5 based on the second cell in each row.

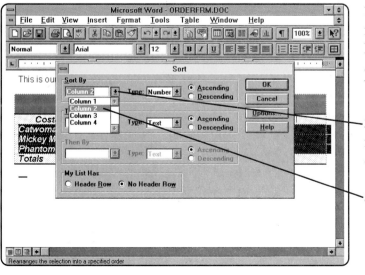

1. **Repeat steps 1 through 4** in the previous section to **highlight rows 3 through 5** and to **open** the **Sort dialog box**.

2. **Click** on the ⬇ to the right of Sort By. A pull-down list will appear.

3. **Click** on **Column 2**.

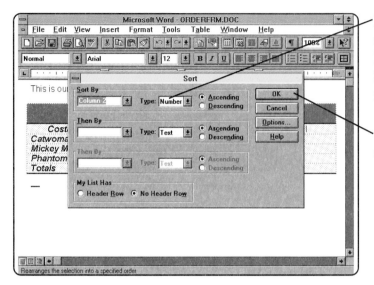

Notice that Word has changed the type to Number in the Type box because it knew there were numbers in column 2.

4. **Click** on **OK** to start the sorting process.

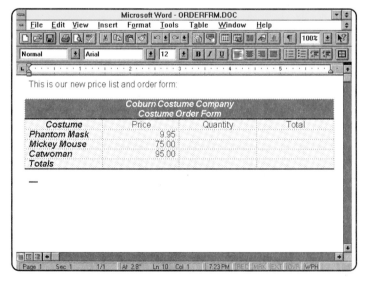

5. **Click anywhere** to remove the highlighting.

Your screen will look like this.

UNDOING A SORT

You can undo a sort with the click of your mouse. But be sure *not to perform any other function* between the numeric sort and the Undo or else it won't work. In this example you will undo the numerical sort you just applied in the previous section and return to the alphabetic sort.

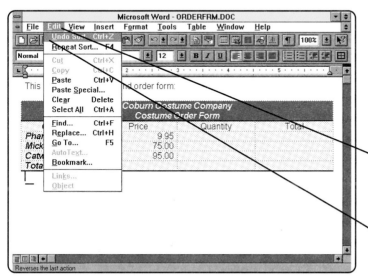

1. Click on **Edit** in the menu bar. A pull-down menu will appear.

2. Click on **Undo Sort**.

ADDING A ROW

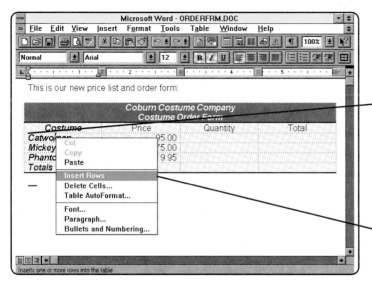

You can add a row anywhere in the table. In this example you will add a row above row 3.

1. Click on **Catwoman** in **row 3** to place the cursor.

2. Click the **right mouse button**. A quick menu will appear.

3. Click on **Insert Rows**. A row will be added to the table above row 3.

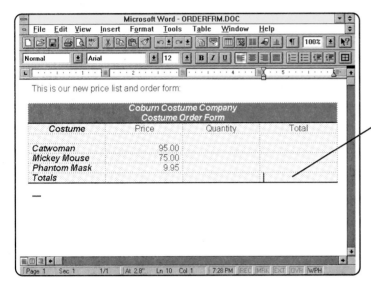

If you think adding a row in the middle of a table was easy, wait until you see how easily you can add a row to the end of a table.

4. Click in the **last cell** of the table to place the cursor.

5. Press the **Tab key**. Another row will be added to the end of the table. (Remember, if you press the Enter key you will increase the height of the current row.)

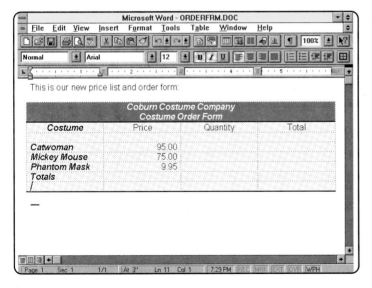

Your table will look like this.

DELETING A ROW

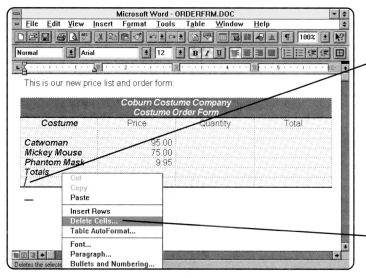

You can delete a row as easily as you added one.

1. Click in the row you want to delete. In this example, click in the **last row** if your cursor is not already there.

2. Click the **right mouse button**. A quick menu will appear.

3. Click on **Delete Cells**. The Delete Cells dialog box will appear.

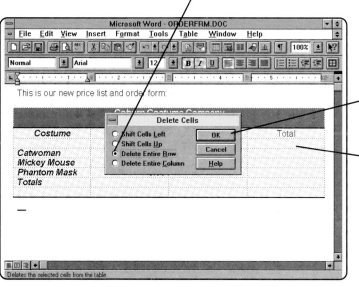

4. Click on **Delete Entire Row** to insert a dot in the circle. (To delete the column where the cursor is placed you would click on Delete Entire Column.)

5. Click on **OK**. The row will be deleted.

6. Repeat steps 1 through 5 to delete the third row.

ADDING A COLUMN

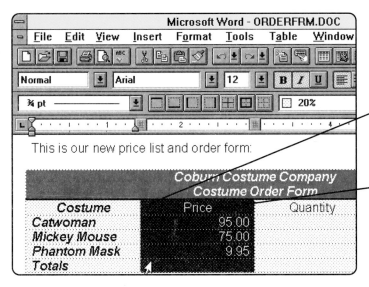

Word will add a column to the left of a selected column. First, you have to highlight the entire column.

1. Position the mouse pointer in the **Price cell** so that it is an arrow.

2. Press and hold the mouse button and **drag** the arrow and the highlight bar down to the **last row** in column B.

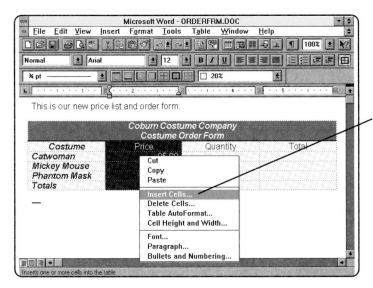

3. Keep the pointer in the **highlighted area** and **press** the *right* **mouse button**. A quick menu will appear.

4. Click on **Insert Cells**. The Insert Cells dialog box will appear.

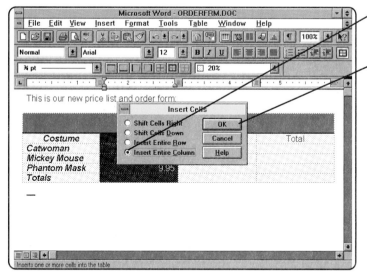

5. Click on **Insert Entire Column**.

6. Click on **OK**. A column the width of the highlighted column will be inserted to the left. The new column will contain the same formatting that was applied to the highlighted column. For example, the new cell B2 will center whatever you enter into the cell. You can, of course, change the formatting.

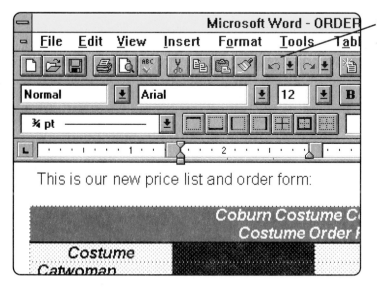

7. Click on the **Undo button** to remove the new column.

CHANGING COLUMN WIDTH

There are several ways to change the width of your columns. In the following section you will use two different methods to change the width of a column.

1. Click anywhere in the **table**.

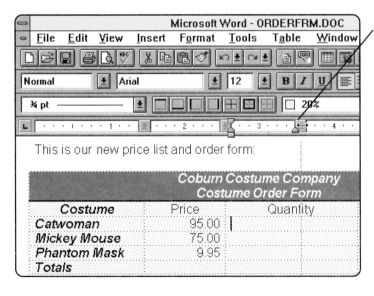

2. Place the mouse arrow on top of the **right boundary line for column 2** so that your mouse pointer turns into the symbol you see here. You will probably have to fiddle with the cursor to get it into the right shape.

3. Press and hold the mouse button and **drag** the **dotted line** to the **2½ inch mark** on the ruler bar. Then **release** the mouse button. The second column will now be 1 inch wide.

4. Place the mouse arrow on top of the **column 3 column marker**. Your pointer will turn into a double arrow.

5. Press and hold the mouse button and **drag** the **column marker** to the **3½ inch mark** on the ruler bar. Then **release** the mouse button. The third column will now be 1 inch wide.

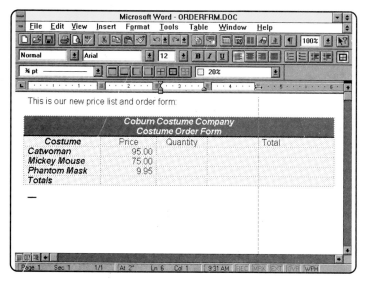

Notice that the table has remained the same overall size and only the widths of columns B and C have changed. Now you will adjust the right edge of the table and change its size.

6. Use one of the methods just shown and **drag** the **right table boundary line** to the **4½ inch mark** on the ruler bar.

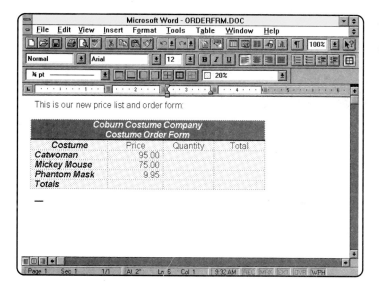

Your table will look like this example.

UNDOING AND REDOING MULTIPLE STEPS

Word keeps track of the changes you make. You can use the Multiple Undo feature to undo up to six previous steps! In this example you will undo the three changes you just made to column widths.

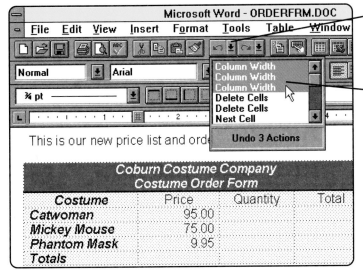

1. Click on the ⬇ to the right of the Undo button. A pull-down list will appear.

2. Click and hold on the **first Column Width** and **drag** the highlight bar down to the **third Column Width**. When you release the mouse button the list will disappear and the last three column width changes you made will be undone.

You can even redo a multiple undo! (Don't you wish life was so forgiving.)

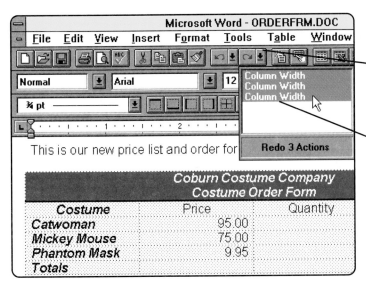

3. Click on the ⬇ to the right of the Redo button. A pull-down list will appear.

4. Click on the **first Column Width** and **drag** the highlight bar down to the **third Column Width**. Then **release** the mouse button to redo the width changes.

CENTERING THE TABLE

When Word first creates a table, it extends the table the width of the page. When you change column width Word keeps the same left margin. This often means that the table is no longer centered across the page. But you can center it very easily.

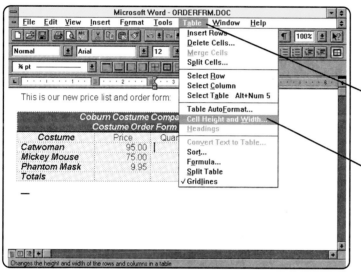

1. **Click anywhere** in the table if your cursor is not already there.

2. **Click** on **Table** in the menu bar. A pull-down menu will appear.

3. **Click** on **Cell Height and Width**. The Cell Height and Width dialog box will appear.

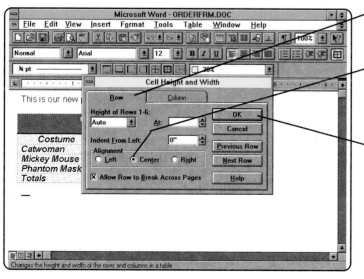

4. **Click** on the **Row tab** to go to the Row dialog box.

5. **Click** on **Center** under Alignment to insert a dot into the circle.

6. **Click** on **OK**. The dialog box will close and your table will now be centered across the page.

Your document will look like this example.

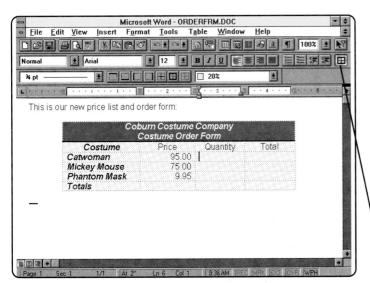

ADDING GRIDLINES FOR PRINTING

The gridlines you see on the screen will not print. If you want gridlines on the printed document, you have to add them.

1. **Click** on the **Borders button** the toolbar. The Border toolbar will appear on your screen.

Now you have to select the entire table in order to apply inside and outside border lines.

2. **Click anywhere** in the table to place the cursor.

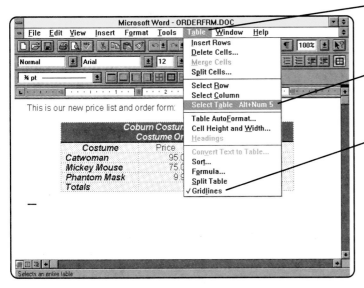

3. **Click** on **Table** in the menu bar. A pull-down list will appear.

4. **Click** on **Select Table**. The entire table will be highlighted.

The ✔ next to Gridlines means that gridlines show on the screen. It has nothing to do with the printed page. Clicking on Gridlines, would remove the ✔ and the gridlines would not show on the screen.

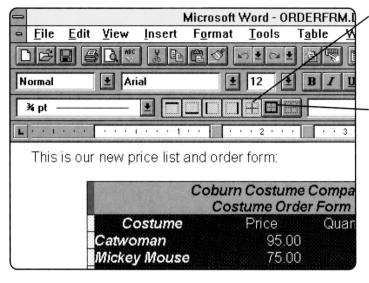

5. **Click** on the **Inside Border button** on the Border toolbar to put lines inside the table.

6. **Click** on the **Outside Border button** on the Border toolbar to put lines on the outside of the table.

7. **Click anywhere** to remove the highlighting and see the lines.

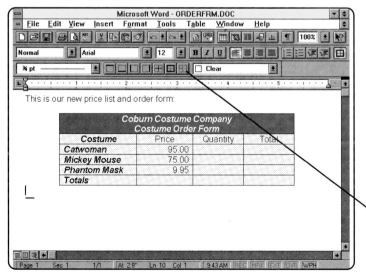

REMOVING THE LINES FROM THE PRINTED PAGE

1. **Repeat steps 2 through 4** in the previous section to select the entire table.

2. **Click** on the **No Border button** on the Border toolbar to remove the inside and outside lines.

DELETING AND UNDELETING A TABLE

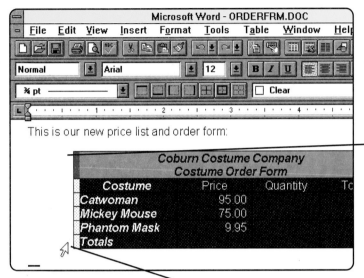

Deleting and undeleting a table is as easy as deleting and undeleting text. In this example you will delete the table in the ORDERFRM document.

1. Click outside the table next to the first line. The cursor will be in the shape of an arrow. The line will be highlighted.

2. Press and hold the mouse button and **drag** the arrow down to the end of the table. The entire table will be highlighted. (This is another way to select the entire table.)

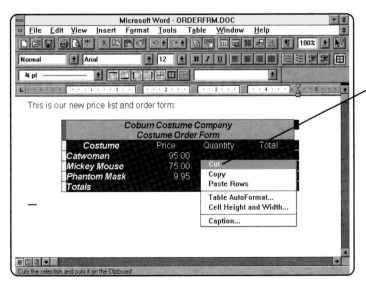

3. Click the *right* mouse **button**. A quick menu will appear.

4. Click on **Cut**. The table will be deleted from the document.

5. If you want to restore the table to your screen, **click** on the **Undo button** before you do any other function.

6. Save the changes if you want to keep the table.

Copying a Table From a Worksheet

As is the case with all Windows programs, there are several ways to do any given task. One way to insert a spreadsheet table into Word is to copy the table in the spreadsheet program and then paste it into Word. Once the table is in Word, you can edit and format it like any other table.

This chapter will use Excel as the spreadsheet program. The process is similar in other spreadsheet programs. In this chapter you will do the following:

❖ Copy a spreadsheet created in Excel

❖ Paste the spreadsheet into Word

SETTING UP A WORD DOCUMENT

Before you start this chapter, complete the following steps:

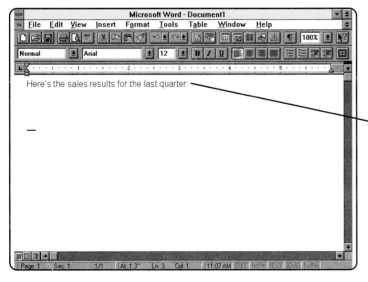

❖ Open your worksheet program

❖ Open the worksheet you want to copy

1. **Type** the sentence **"Here's the sales results for the last quarter."**

2. **Press Enter twice** to move the cursor where you want to insert an Excel Table.

SWITCHING TO EXCEL

1. **Click** on the **Control Menu box** (⊟). A pull-down menu will appear.

2. **Click** on **Switch To**. The Task List dialog box will appear.

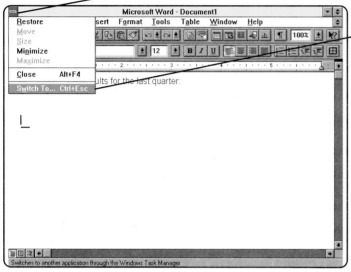

The list of files you see in your Task List dialog box may be different from the ones you see here. The Task List shows the programs that are currently running on your computer.

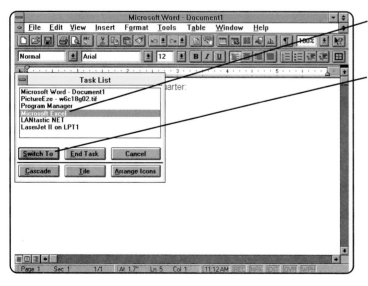

3. **Click** on **Microsoft Excel** to highlight it.

4. **Click** on **Switch To**. The Task List dialog box will disappear and Microsoft Excel will appear on your screen.

COPYING THE TABLE

You can copy the table just as you would copy text in Word.

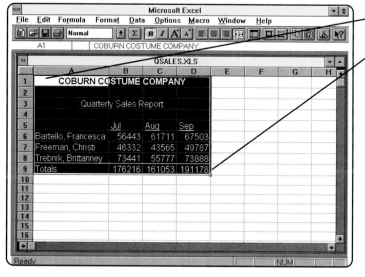

1. **Click** on **A1**.

2. **Press and hold** the mouse button as you **drag** the cursor down and to the right to highlight the **table** you want to insert.

3. **Release** the mouse button.

4. **Click** on **Edit** in the menu bar. A pull-down menu will appear.

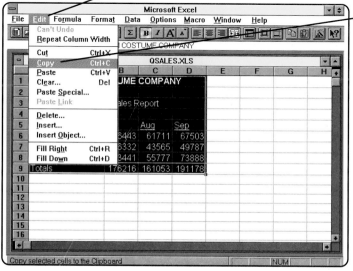

5. **Click** on **Copy**. The table you highlighted will be copied to the Windows clipboard.

SWITCHING TO WORD

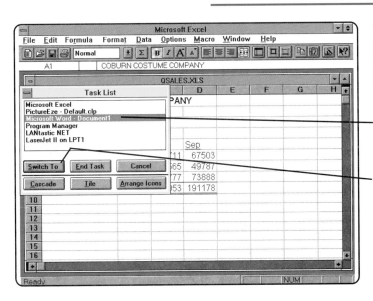

1. Press and hold the **Ctrl key** and then **press** the **Esc key**. The Task List dialog box will appear.

2. Click on **Microsoft Word** to highlight it.

3. Click on **Switch To**. The Task List dialog box will disappear and Word will appear on your screen.

INSERTING THE TABLE INTO WORD

1. Click on **Edit** in the menu bar. A pull-down menu will appear.

2. Click on **Past Special**. The Paste Special dialog box will appear.

3. **Click** on **Formatted Text (RTF)** to highlight it.

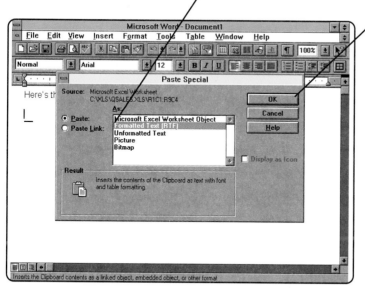

4. **Click** on **OK**. The Paste Special dialog box will disappear and the table you copied will be pasted into your Word document at the insertion point. You can now edit, format, and print the table as part of the Word document.

CLOSING WORD

1. **Click twice** on the **Control Menu box** (⊟). A Microsoft Word dialog box will appear.

2. **Click** on **No**.

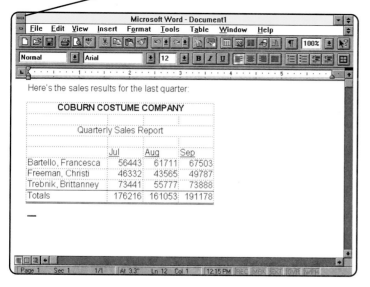

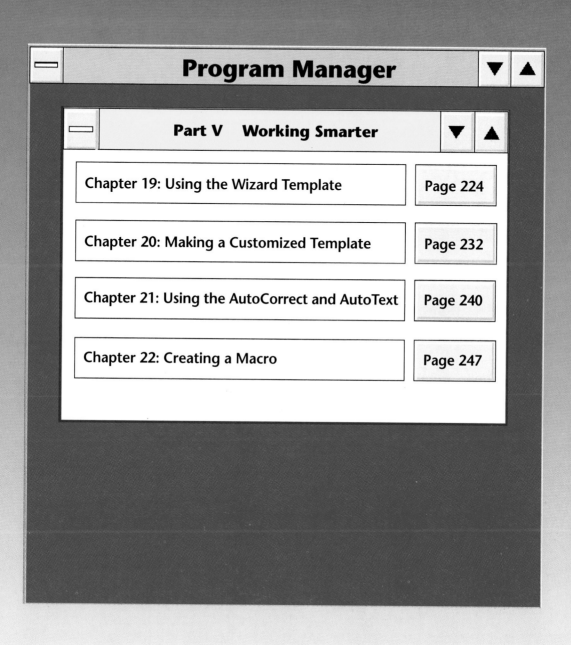

Program Manager

Part V   Working Smarter

Using the Wizard Template

A template is a basic outline of a letter, memo, report or other word processing document that you use over and over again. For example, if you write a memorandum to your staff monthly, you may want to use a customized template that you update each month. Word 6 has two types of templates. The standard template is one that you edit like any other document on the screen. The second type is called a Wizard template. A Wizard template allows you to customize and edit the document you are creating from it with a series of dialog boxes. Using templates helps you work faster by saving time laying out a document and entering text into it. In Chapter 20 you will customize a standard template. In this chapter, you will do the following:

* Set up a Wizard template
* Print a Wizard product

SELECTING A WIZARD TEMPLATE

1. **Click** on **File**. A pull-down menu will appear.

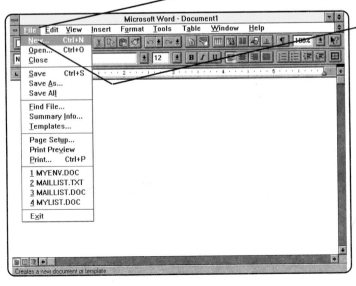

2. **Click** on **New**. The New dialog box will appear. It will show a list of standard and Wizard templates in the Template list box.

3. Click on **Award Wizard**. Award Wizard will move to the Filename text box.

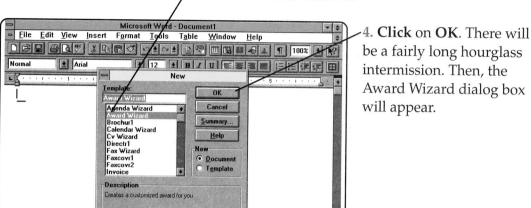

4. Click on **OK**. There will be a fairly long hourglass intermission. Then, the Award Wizard dialog box will appear.

FILLING IN THE TEXT

Notice that there are four award layout options. You can view them in this dialog box by clicking on the circle next to the option. The certificate will appear in the preview box.

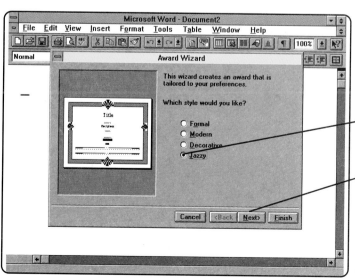

1. Click on **Jazzy**, to place a dot in the circle.

2. Click on **Next>**. Another Award Wizard dialog box will appear.

Notice that Landscape printing (also known as sideways printing) is selected. This means that the printing will be done with the long side of the paper at the top. If you choose portrait orientation (which is normally how most letters are printed) the short side of the paper is at the top.

Notice also that Award Wizard is set up to print on paper without a border. You can, of course, click on Yes if your paper has a border.

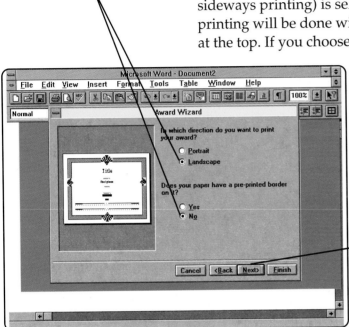

3. **Click** on **Next>**. Another Award Wizard dialog box will appear.

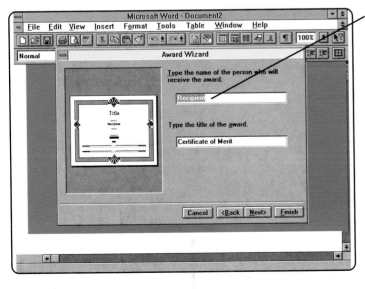

4. **Click** to the **right** of the letter **"t"** in the word Recipient to set the cursor.

5. **Press and hold** the mouse button as you **drag** to the left to highlight the word **"Recipient." Release** the mouse button.

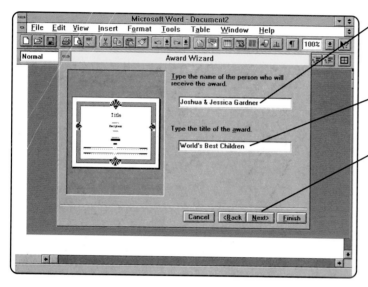

6. Type the **name** of the person (or persons) receiving the award.

7. Repeat steps 4 to 6 to fill in the title of the award.

8. Click on **Next>**. Another Award Wizard dialog box will appear.

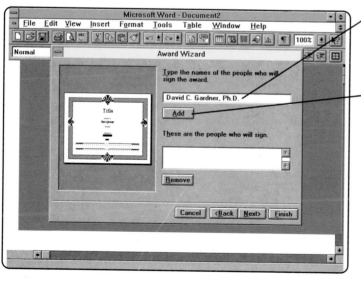

9. Repeat steps 4 to 6 to type the name of the first person signing the award.

10. Click on **Add**. The typed name will move to the "These are the people who will sign" List box.

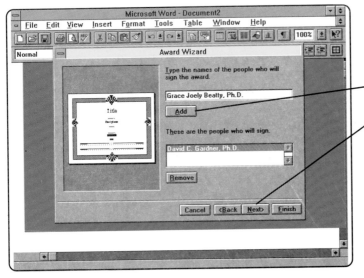

11. Repeat steps 4 to 6 to type the name of the second signer of the award.

12. Click on **Add**.

13. Click on **Next>**.

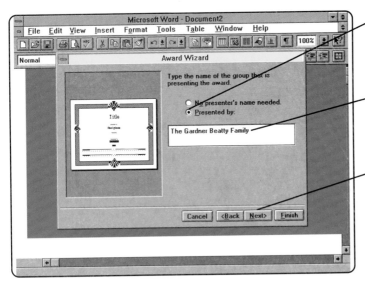

14. Click on the **circle** to the **left** of Presented by to place a dot in it.

15. Repeat steps 4 to 6 to type the name of the group that is presenting the award.

16. Click on **Next>**.

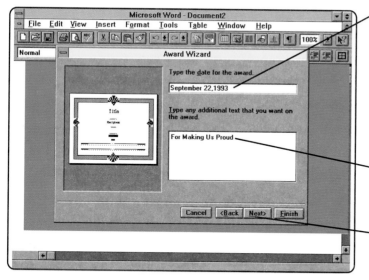

Notice that the current date is automatically selected in the text box.

17. Repeat steps 4 through 6 if you want to change the date. If not, go to step 18.

18. Repeat steps 4 through 6 to type any additional text.

19. Click on **Next>**.

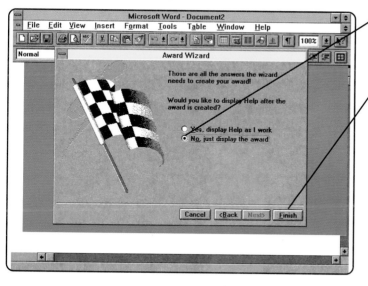

20. Click on the **circle** next to No to put a black dot in it.

21. Click on **Finish**. After a brief hourglass intermission, the completed certificate will appear on your screen. Wow!

PREVIEWING THE WIZARD PRODUCT

1. **Click** on **File** in the menu bar. A pull-down menu will appear.

2. **Click** on **Print Preview**.

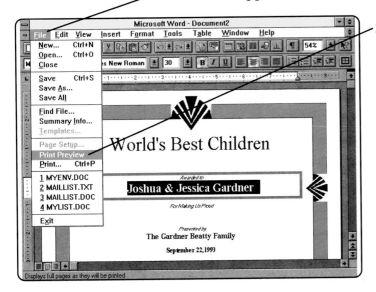

PRINTING THE WIZARD PRODUCT

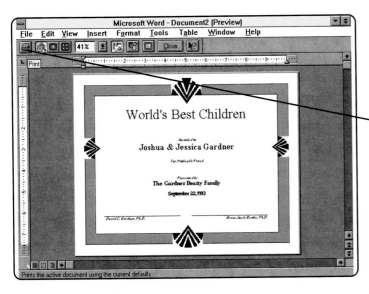

1. **Click** on the **Print button** in the toolbar. After awhile, the certificate will print.

CLOSING THE WIZARD TEMPLATE

1. **Click twice** on the **Control Menu box** on the menu bar. A Microsoft Word dialog box will appear.

2. **Click** on **No**. If you need to revise this certificate Award Wizard will automatically come up in the same format the next time you select it. You will need to open Award Wizard, again, and click on Next to find the screen that you want to change.

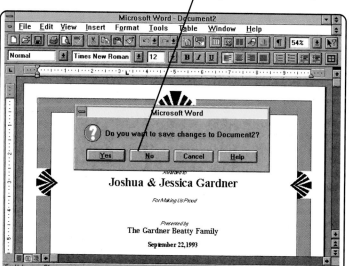

You now are ready to go on to the next chapter.

Making a Customized Template

A template is a basic outline of a letter, memo, report or other word processing document that you use over and over again. For example, if you write a memorandum to your staff monthly, you may want to use a customized template that you update each month. Word 6 has two types of templates. The standard template is one that you edit like any other document on the screen. The second type is called a Wizard template. A Wizard template allows you to customize and edit the document you are creating from it with a series of dialog boxes. If you want to learn how to use a Wizard, see Chapter 19. Using templates helps you work faster by saving time laying out a document and entering text into it. In this chapter, you will do the following:

❖ Open a template
❖ Save As a new template
❖ Add a graphic
❖ Customize the text

OPENING A STANDARD TEMPLATE

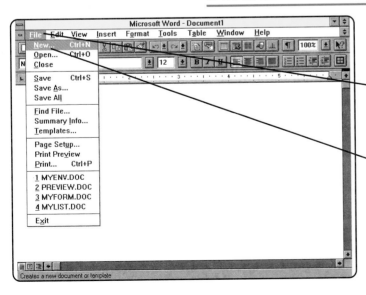

1. **Open** a **new document** if one is not already open.

2. **Click** on **File** in the menu bar. A pull-down menu will appear.

3. **Click** on **New**. The New dialog box will appear.

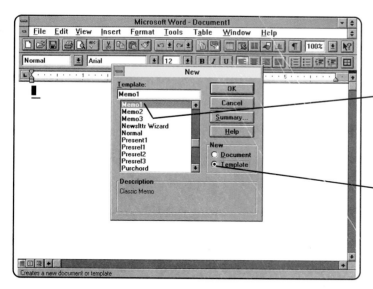

4. Click repeatedly on the ⬇ to scroll down the list of templates and Wizards.

5. Click on **Memo1** to highlight it. Memo1 will move to the Template name text box.

6. Click on the **circle** to the **left** of **Template** to put a dot in the circle.

7. Click on **OK**. Template1 will appear on our screen.

SAVING THE FILE AS A NEW TEMPLATE

1. Click on **File** in the menu bar. A pull-down menu will appear.

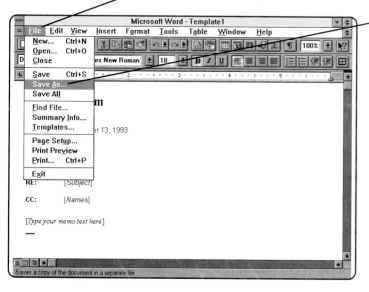

2. Click on **Save As**. The Save As dialog box will appear.

3. **Type salesmem** in the File Name text box.

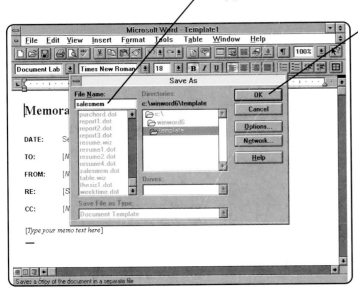

4. **Click** on **OK**. The file will be saved as the Salesmem.dot template. You are now ready to modify the new template. (The template has not changed).

ADDING A GRAPHIC
TO THE TEMPLATE

1. **Click** on the **Page Layout button** in the lower-left corner of your screen. The screen will change to a layout view where it is easier to see the graph in relation to the text.

Notice that the cursor is flashing before the word Memorandum.

2. **Press** the **Enter key** twice to move the word Memorandum down two lines to make room for a graphic.

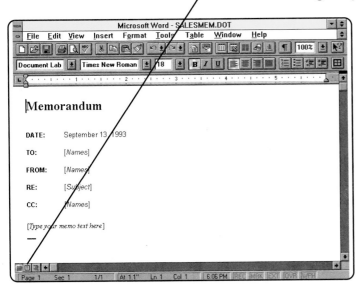

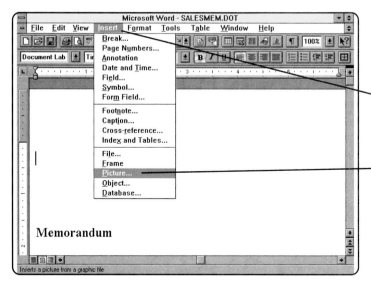

3. **Press** the ↑ on your keyboard twice to move the cursor up two lines.

4. **Click** on **Insert** in the menu bar. A pull-down menu will appear.

5. **Click** on **Picture**. The Insert Picture dialog box will appear.

6. **Click repeatedly** on the ⬇ to the right of the File Name list box to scroll down the list.

7. **Click** on **theatre.wmf**. It will move to the File Name list box.

8. **Click** on **OK**. The theatre picture will appear on your screen.

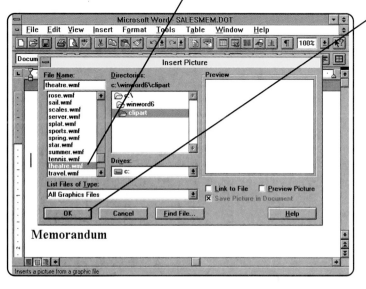

Changing the View

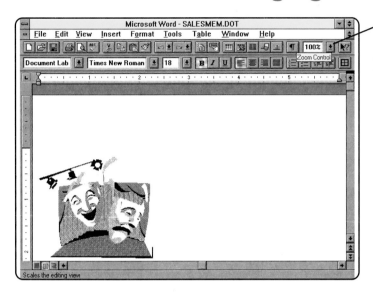

1. **Click** on the **Zoom control** ⬇. A drop-down list will appear.

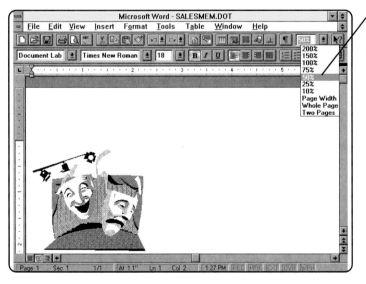

2. **Click** on **50%**. The picture (theatre.wmf) can now be viewed easier in relation to the text.

Sizing the Graphic

1. **Click** on the **graphic**. It will be surrounded by a black border with handles.

2. **Move** the **mouse arrow** to the **lower-right corner**. It will turn into a 2 headed arrow.

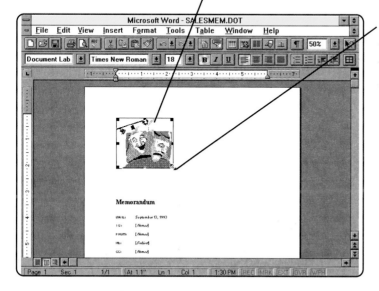

3. **Press and hold** the mouse arrow as you **move** it up and to the left. A dotted box will appear. It represents the "new" size of the graphic as you size it.

4. **Release** the mouse button when you think the new size is about right. You may have to fiddle with it to get it the way you want.

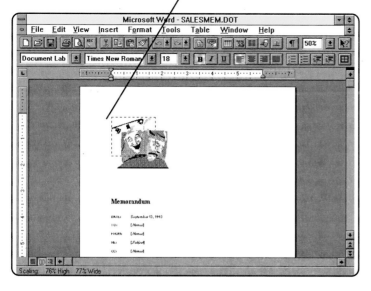

ENTERING A BOILER PLATE TEXT

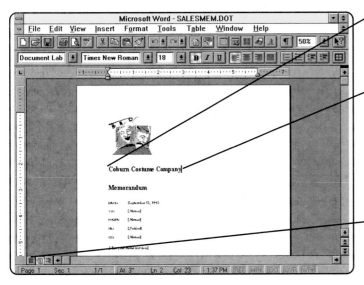

1. Click the **mouse arrow** below the graphic to set the cursor.

2. Type Coburn Costume Company. Notice the type style is automatically the same as "Memorandum" ("Times New Roman, 18pts, Bold).

3. Click on the **Normal View button** to return to the faster text editing mode.

4. Click repeatedly on the ⬇ on the right scroll bar to bring the rest of the text into view.

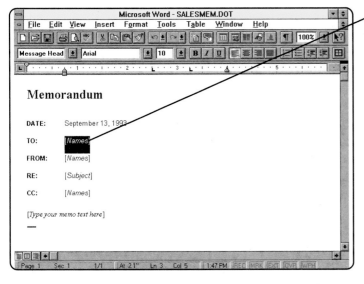

5. Click to the **right** of {Names} on the "To" line to set the cursor.

6. Press and hold as you **drag** to the left to highlight the text. **Release** the mouse button.

7. **Type WEST COAST SALES GROUP**.

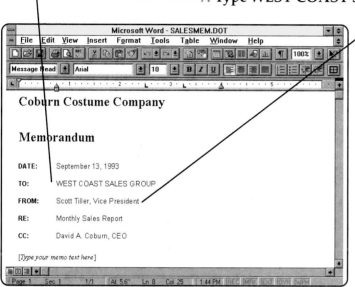

8. **Repeat steps 3 to 6** to type the following:

Scott Tiller, Vice President
Monthly Sales Report
David A. Coburn, CEO

SAVING AND CLOSING THE TEMPLATE

1. **Click** on the **Save button**.

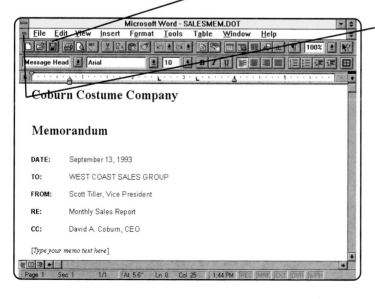

2. **Click twice** on the **Control Menu box** in the menu bar.

Using AutoCorrect and AutoText

Most people have text or graphics that they use over and over again. Word has two ways you can store these frequently used items so that you can insert them into your document quickly. The first is Autotext which allows you to insert a word of phrase or graphic into your document by typing a few key strokes, clicking a button or using a command. AutoCorrect allows you to insert an item as you type without clicking a button or using a command. In this chapter you will do the following:

❖ Setup and use an AutoText entry

❖ Setup and use an AutoCorrect entry

USING AUTOTEXT

AutoText is an excellent program for storing and inserting text, graphics, or other items that you use once in a while, such as the closing to a letter. You may also want to use AutoText for items that you do not want to insert automatically as you type.

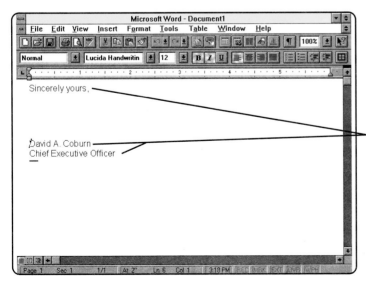

Creating an AutoText Entry

1. Type a **closing** that you use for your letters. In this example we used a closing for David A. Coburn, Chief Executive Officer.

2. **Click** to the **left** of the **"S"** in Sincerely to set the cursor.

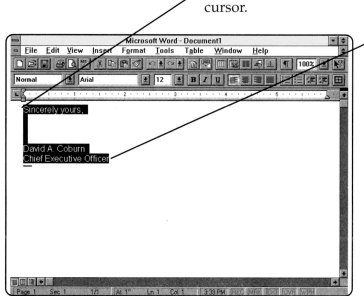

3. **Press and hold** the mouse button as you **drag** it down and to the right to highlight the closing text.

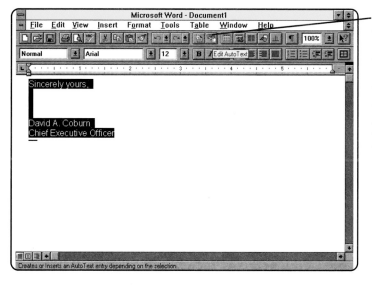

4. **Click** on the **AutoText button** on the toolbar. The AutoText dialog box will appear. "Sincerely yours, David A. Coburn, Chief Executive Officer" will be highlighted in the Name text box.

5. **Type** "closing".

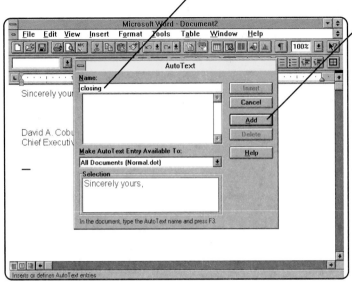

6. **Click** on **Add**. The closing will move to the list of AutoText items so fast that you can't see it. The document screen will reappear.

Inserting an AutoText Item

1. **Click anywhere** on the document white space to clear the highlight.

2. **Press** the **Enter key twice** to move the cursor down two lines.

3. **Click** on the **Insert AutoText button** on the toolbar. The AutoText dialog box will appear.

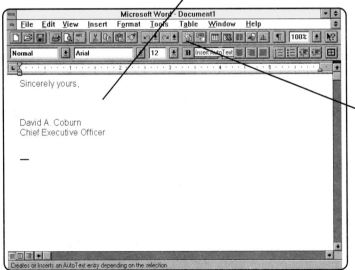

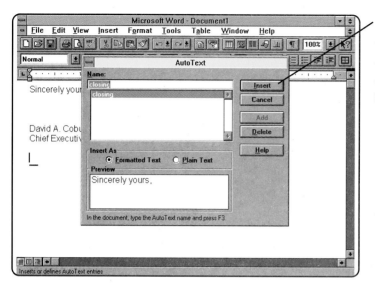

4. Click on **Insert**. The dialog box will disappear and the closing text will appear on the document. Slick!

CREATING AN AUTOCORRECT ENTRY

1. Press the **Enter key twice** to move down two lines.

2. Type "Call me."

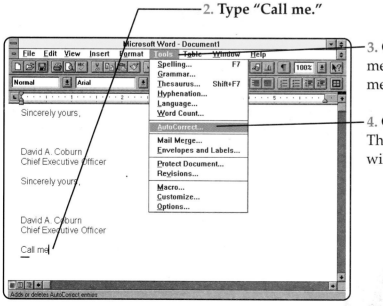

3. Click on **Tools** in the menu bar. A pull-down menu will appear.

4. Click on **AutoCorrect**. The AutoCorrect dialog box will appear.

5. **Type "asap"** in the Replace text box.

6. **Press** the **Tab key**.

7. **Type "as soon as possible"** in the With text box.

8. **Click** on **Add**.

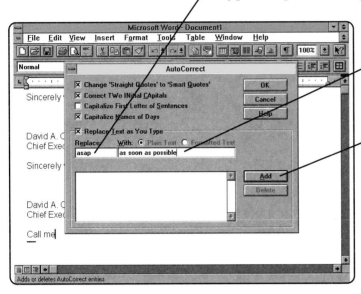

Notice that the text "asap" and the text to replace it is highlighted.

9. **Click** on **OK**. Document1 will reappear.

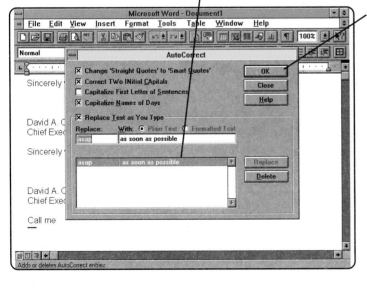

Inserting An AutoCorrect Item

1. Press the **Spacebar once** and **type "asap."**

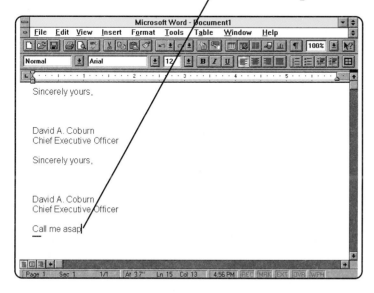

2. Press the **Spacebar once**. Zap! "Asap" is replaced by the new text. Even slicker!

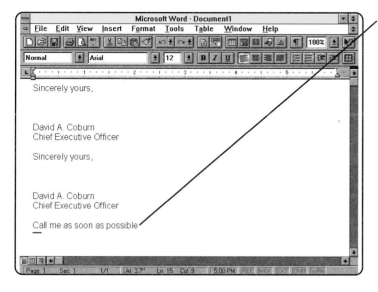

CLOSING DOCUMENT1

1. Click twice on the **Control Menu box** on the title bar. A Microsoft Word dialog box will appear.

2. Click on **No**.

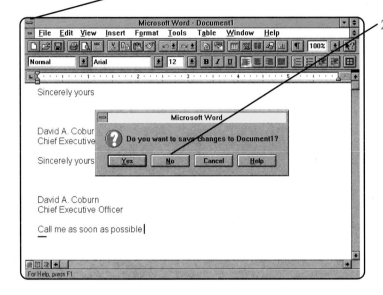

Creating a Macro

Creating a macro is a way to consolidate a series of commands into a single command. Carefully thought out macros can make everyday word processing tasks easier and faster. In Word 6, you can assign a macro to a menu, a tool bar, or shortcut keys. In this chapter you will do the following:

❖ Open the Macro Recorder

❖ Assign the macro command to the File menu bar

❖ Record the macro

❖ Use the macro

❖ Delete the macro

SETTING UP THE MACRO

In this example you will create a simple macro. We urge you to go through these steps as a trial run before creating your own customized macro. It is very important to plan ahead when creating your own macros to avoid panicsville.

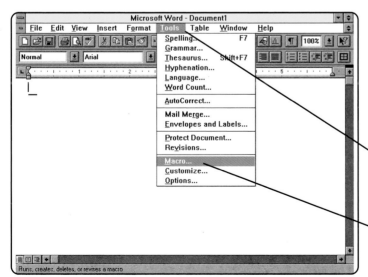

Opening the Macro Recorder

1. **Click** on **Tools** in the menu bar. A drop-down list of files will appear.

2. **Click** on **Macro**. The Macro dialog box will appear.

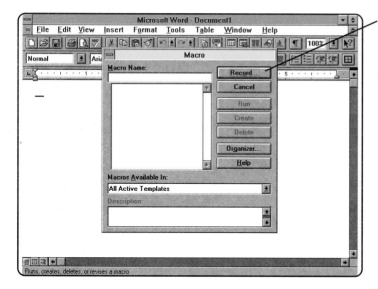

3. Click on **Record**. The Record Macro dialog box will appear. Macro1 will be highlighted in the Record Macro Name text box.

ASSIGNING THE MACRO COMMAND LOCATION

1. Type "Opening Sales Memo Template" in the Description text box.

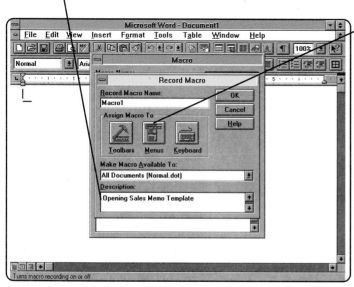

2. Click on the **Menus button** in the Assign Macro To box. The Customize dialog box will appear.

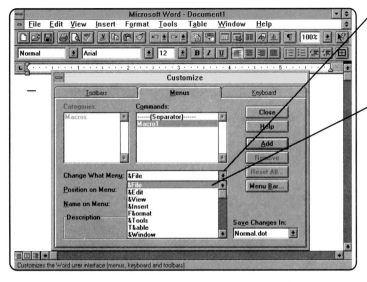

3. **Click** on ▼ to the right of the Change What Menu list box. A drop-down list will appear.

4. **Click** on the menu option, **&File**. The menu option &File will appear highlighted in the Change What Menu list box.

5. **Press Tab**. The option, (Auto) will be highlighted in the Position on Menu list box.

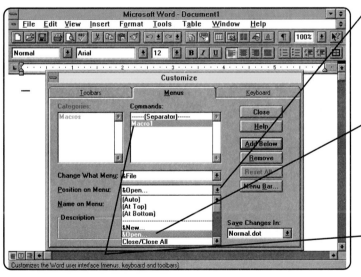

6. **Click** on the ▼ to the right of the Position on Menu list box. A drop-down list of menu locations will appear.

7. **Click** on the menu option, **&Open**. The menu option, &Open will appear in the Position on Menu List box.

8. **Press Tab**. The menu option, &Macro1 in the Name on Menu list box will be highlighted.

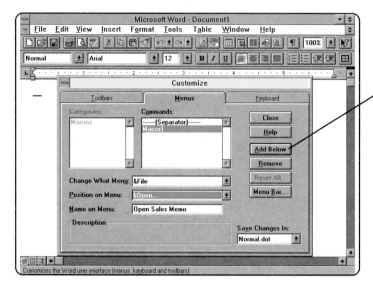

9. **Type "Open Sales Memo"** in the Name on Menu box.

10. **Click** on **Add Below**. Open Sales Memo will appear in the Position on Menu list box.

Recording the Macro

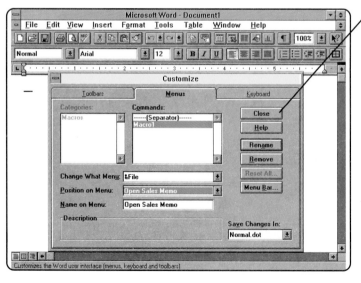

1. **Click** on **Close**. The document1 screen will appear. The mouse pointer will have a graphic attached to it. The Macro Record toolbar will appear.

Notice the Macro Record Toolbar.

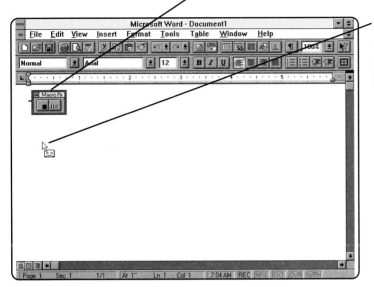

Notice the Mouse pointer with the Record Graphic. It may appear in a different location on your screen.

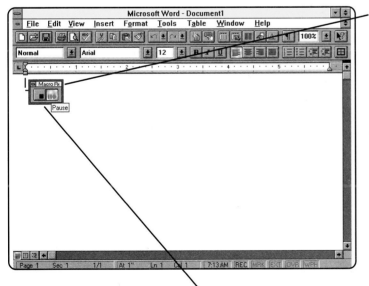

Notice that you can temporarily stop the recording process by clicking the pause button on the right side of the toolbar. The pause button allows you to move around the document and make any keystrokes without making them a part of the macro. When you are ready to begin recording the macro again, click on the pause button.

Warning: Do not click on the stop button (left) on the toolbar until you have finished recording all of the steps you want in the macro. Once you click on the stop button the macro is terminated and you may be macroed for life!

Notice that the new macro command appears on the menu where you placed it. However, the macro *is not* complete until you finish the steps and click on the stop button.

2. **Click** on **File** in the menu bar. A pull-down menu will appear.

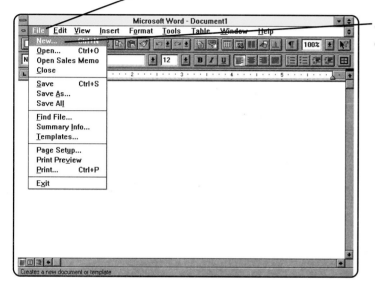

3. **Click** on **New**. The New dialog box will appear.

4. **Click** on the ⬇ to scroll down the list of templates.

5. **Click twice** on **Salesmem**. The SALESMEM document will appear on the screen as Document2.

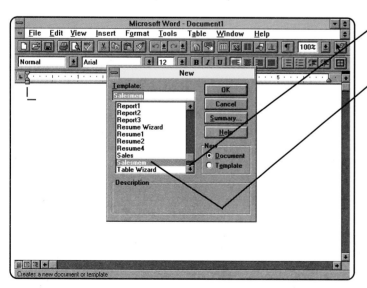

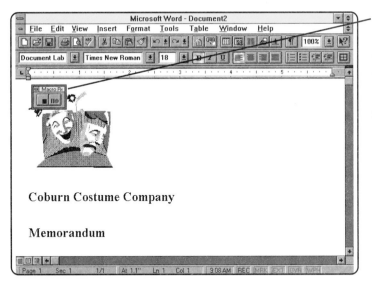

6. Click on the **Stop button** on the Macro Recorder toolbar. The Macro Recorder toolbar will disappear. All of the steps in the macro are now recorded.

USING THE MACRO

1. Click twice on the **Control Menu box** in the menu bar to close Document2. The Document1 screen will appear.

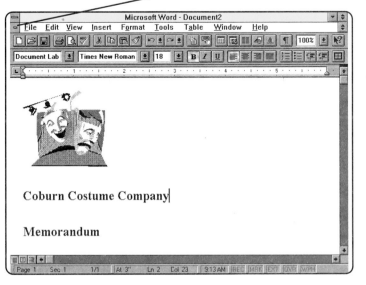

2. **Click** on **File** in the menu bar. A pull-down menu will appear.

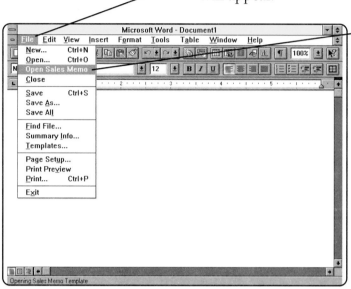

3. **Click** on **Open Sales Memo**. The Sales Memo will appear as Document2, ready for editing. Wow!

DELETING THE MACRO

1. **Click** on **Tools** in the menu bar. A pull-down menu will appear.

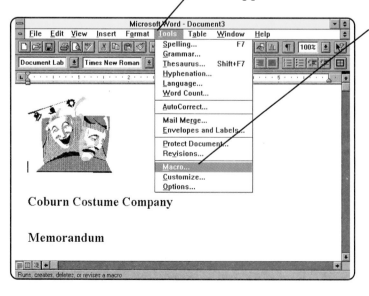

2. **Click** on **Macro**. The Macro dialog box will appear.

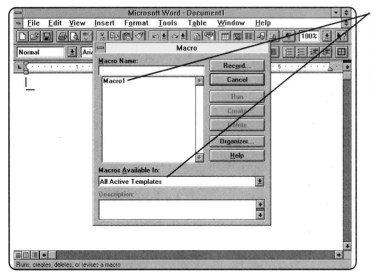

3. Click on **Macro1**. It will move to the Macro Name text box. The description of the Macro will appear in the Description text box.

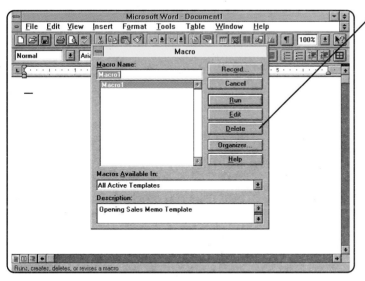

4. Click on **Delete**. A Microsoft Word dialog box will appear.

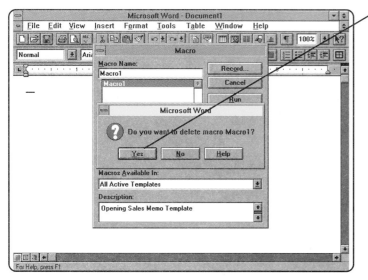

5. Click on **Yes**. The Macro dialog box will appear.

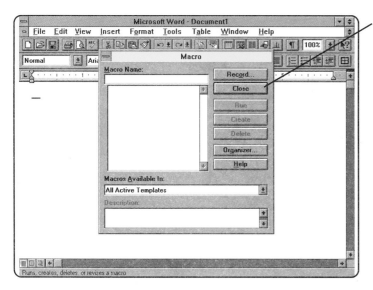

6. Click on **Close**. The Document1 screen will reappear.

EXITING WORD

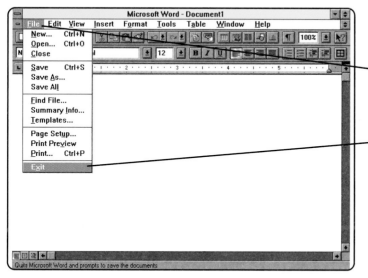

Notice the Open Sales Memo is no longer here.

1. **Click** on **File** on the menu bar. A pull-down menu will appear.

2. **Click** on **Exit**.

WHAT NEXT?

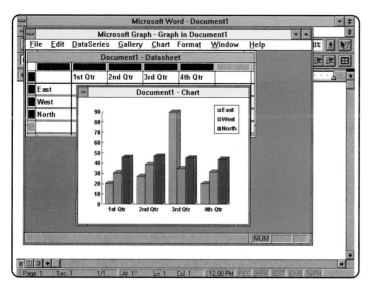

There are many exciting features of Word 6 left to explore. We hope this introduction has given you an understanding of its capabilities. We hope, also, that you have gained confidence in your ability to master its complexities. Experiment! Have fun!

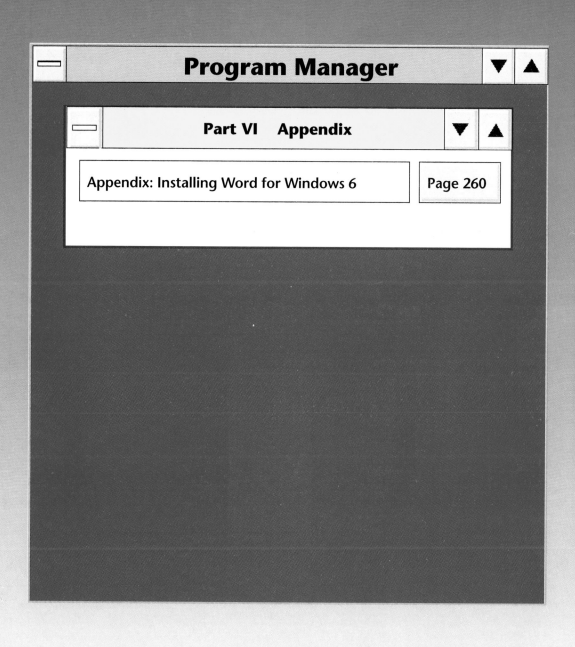

Program Manager

Part VI   Appendix

Appendix: Installing Word for Windows 6 | Page 260

Installing Word for Windows 6

This appendix will describe a standard (typical) installation. If you want to customize your installation, refer to the *Word for Windows 6 Reference Manual*. In this appendix you will do the following:

❖ Install Word 6

Before you start, make sure that you have made and are using backup copies of your Word 6 Install disks. If you need help backing up your disks, see the *Word for Windows 6 Reference Manual*.

INSTALLING WORD FOR WINDOWS 6

1. Open Windows by **typing win** at the DOS prompt (C:\). The Program Manager opening screen will appear. Your screen may look different from this one.

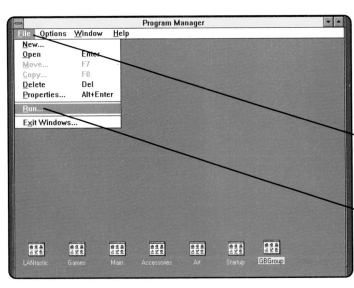

2. Insert your backup copy of Word 6 disk Install 1 into drive A (or B).

3. **Click** on **File** in the menu bar. A pull-down menu will appear.

4. **Click** on **Run**. The Run dialog box will appear.

Notice that the cursor is flashing in the Command Line box. When you start typing, your text will be entered in the box.

5. **Type a:\setup** (or b:\setup).

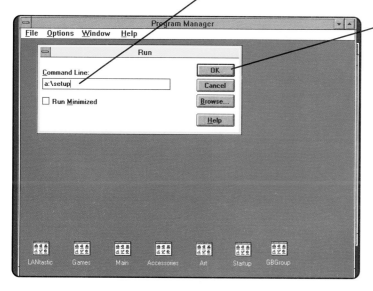

6. **Click** on **OK**. The hourglass will appear briefly with a Word message box that says, "Starting Microsoft Word Setup, please wait." Next, the Microsoft Word 6 Setup dialog box will appear.

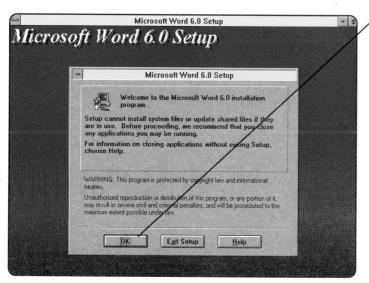

7. **Click** on **OK**. The Name and Organization Information dialog box will appear.

Notice that the cursor is flashing in the Name box. When you start typing, the cursor will disappear.

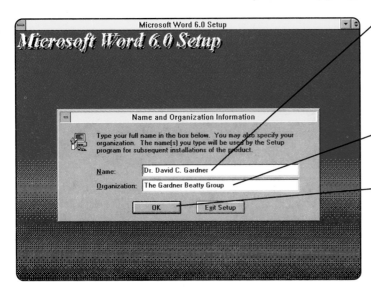

8. **Type** your **full name** in the Name box and then **press Tab** to move the cursor to the Organization text box.

9. **Type** the **name** of your organization.

10. **Click** on **OK**. A second Organization Information dialog box will appear asking you to verify that the information you typed is correct.

11. **Click** on **OK** if the information is correct. The Microsoft Word 6 Setup dialog box will appear.

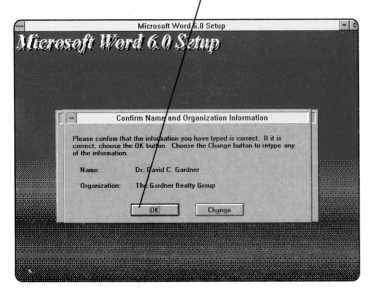

If the information is not correct, click on Change. The previous dialog box will appear. After making your corrections, **click** on **Continue** to return to this dialog box. If you do not type text in the Organization box, the installation will not continue.

The hourglass will appear briefly along with a Word message box that says "Setup is searching for install components."

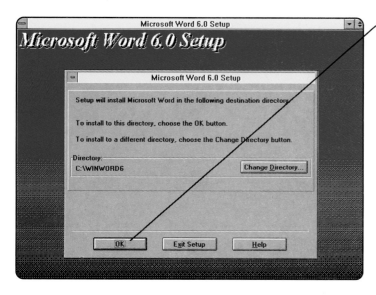

12. **Click** on **OK** if the information is correct.

If you want to change directories, **click** on **Change Directory**. The Change Directory dialog box will appear. Click on ⬇ to scroll down the list of available directories or type in the name of the new directory in the text box and **click** on **OK**.

The hourglass will appear again along with the message "Setup is searching for install components." Next a Microsoft Word 6 Setup dialog box will appear.

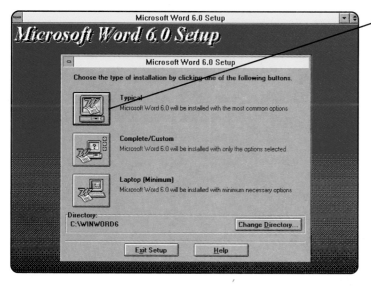

13. **Click** on **Typical** to follow the procedures in this book. Next, the Microsoft Word Choose Program Manager Group dialog box will appear.

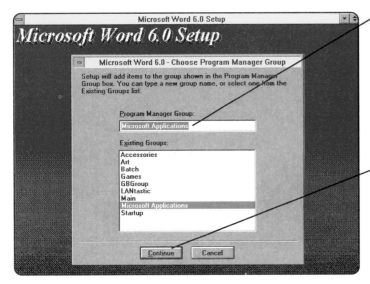

Notice that Microsoft Applications is highlighted in the Program Manager Group text box. If you want to change the selection click on another existing group in the list.

14. **Click** on **Continue**. The Help for WordPerfect Users dialog box will appear.

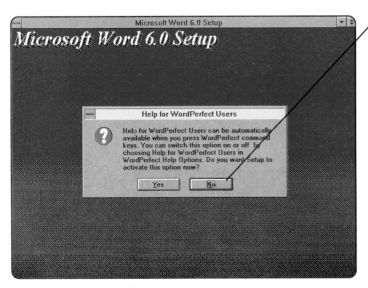

15. **Click** on **No** if you do not want to activate the WordPerfect Help Option. Otherwise, **click** on **Yes**. A message box saying "Space check for necessary diskspace" will briefly appear. Next the Microsoft Word 6 Setup dialog box will appear.

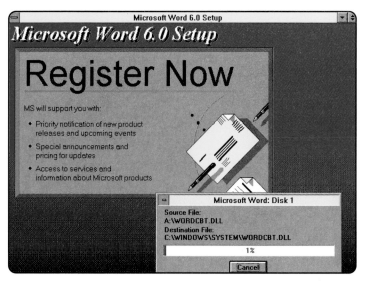

At this point sit back and relax. As you install, watch the background information and pictures in the top half of your screen change as Word is copying the files from the disks to your hard drive. The Microsoft Word dialog box will show you the percent of completion in copying files both for the disk you are currently copying and as a percentage of all the disks.

After Word is done copying the files from the Install 1 disk a Setup Message box will appear.

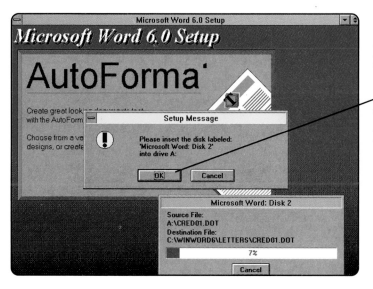

16. Remove Install 1 disk from Drive A and insert the Install 2 disk.

17. Click on **OK**. Word will begin copying the files on Install 2.

Once again the Microsoft Word dialog box will show you the percent of progress.

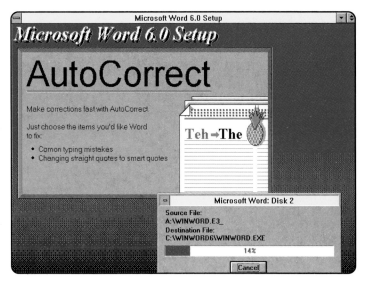

18. **Repeat steps 16 and 17** for disks 2 through 15.

Pay attention to the number on the diskette that Word tells you to insert. Word may skip a disk or two (Word had us skip disk 7 and disk 10, for instance.) Don't be concerned. Word is a "Smart" program and will interact with your specific computer setup as necessary.

Towards the end of installing Disk 15 you will see things happening as Word busies itself with the final stages of the installation. Don't worry! This means you are almost done. Finally the last Microsoft Word 6 Setup dialog will appear indicating a successful installation.

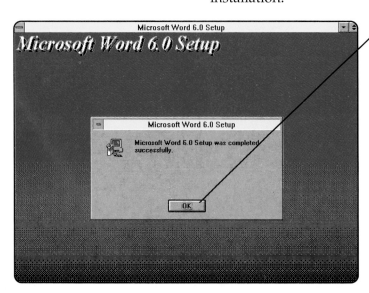

19. **Click** on **OK**. The Word for Windows 6 group window will appear. It may appear in a different size or location than the one shown here.

Congratulations! You have successfully installed Word.

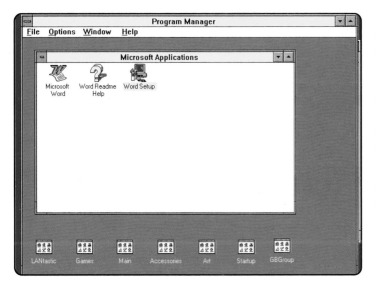

At this point, go to the "Introduction" at the beginning of this book, select your first learning goal, and have fun.

Go to step 3 in Chapter 1, "Changing Margins and Fonts and Entering Text," to start with a screen that looks like this one.

Index

D

Data Source. *See* Mailing lists
Date, entering of, 12
Decimal tabs, 103-105
Defaults
   margins, 5
   for point size, 8
Deleting. *See also* Tables
   macros, 254-256
   page breaks, 111
   rows in tables, 207
   words, deleting and replacing, 48-49
Directories, changing of, 263
Documents. *See also* Editing; Print
     Preview; Saving
   closing documents, 31-32
   deleting/replacing words, 48-49
   naming documents, 20-21
   separating document into two
     sections, 109-111
   switching between open documents,
     106-107
Dot-matrix printers, printing envelopes
     with, 134-136
Dots between words, 11
Double line spacing, 101-102
Drag-and-drop moving, 55-56
Draw program. *See* Line drawing

E

Editing. *See also* Copying and pasting
     text; Page breaks
   AutoCorrect, 243-245
   combining paragraphs, 50-51
   drag-and-drop moving, 55-56
   hard returns, insertion of, 52
   letters and words, adding of, 47-48
   Replace command, 53-54

soft returns, insertion of, 51-52
   tables, 201-216
   undoing edits, 49-50
End mark, 9
Enlarging view in print preview, 25
Entering text, 9-16
Envelopes, xii. *See also* Mailing lists
   attached envelopes, 136-137
     both envelope and letter, printing
      of, 141
     closing without saving, 144
     envelope only, printing of, 142
     letter only, printing of, 143
   bar codes, 131
   boldfacing first line of address, 140
   closing without saving attached
     envelopes, 144
   customizing return address, 136-140
   dot-matrix printers, printing with,
     134-136
   feed position for, 132
   font for return address, changing of,
     129-131
   LaserJet series printers, printing
     with, 133-134
   Mailing Address box, 127-128
   omitting/restoring default return
     address, 132
   opening Envelope dialog box,
     128-129
   style of envelope, changing of,
     137-140
   User Info box for, 126-127
Excel. *See* Worksheets

F

50% zoom, 122
File Name list box, 35
Files. *See* Documents